READINGS IN LENINISM
No. 2

THE THEORY OF THE
PROLETARIAN REVOLUTION

First Published in the United States, 1936

Republished by Red Star Publishers, 2014
www.RedStarPublishers.org

NOTE

This volume is one of a series of "Readings in Leninism." Each book consists of a collection of articles and extracts – taken almost exclusively from the works of Marx, Engels, Lenin and Stalin – dealing with a basic question of Leninist theory.

The key passages included in these volumes are not designed to serve as a substitute for reading the fundamental works of Marxism-Leninism in their entirety. The purpose of the series is to assemble, within the covers of a single book, pertinent excerpts dealing with a specific problem of primary importance, such as the theory of the proletarian revolution, the dictatorship of the proletariat, strategy and tactics of the proletarian revolution, the national and agrarian questions, etc.

Systematically compiled and arranged by V. Bystryansky and M. Mishin, this material should be extremely helpful as a guide to individual or group study of the fundamental principles of Leninism.

The present volume deals with the contradictions of imperialism and the forces of the proletarian revolution; the uneven development of capitalism, and the possibility of the victory of socialism in one country; the main types of revolution in the epoch of imperialism; the growing of the bourgeois-democratic revolution into the proletarian revolution, etc.

CONTENTS

THEORY OF THE PROLETARIAN REVOLUTION

I. CONTRADICTIONS OF IMPERIALISM, PRECONDITIONS AND MOVING FORCES OF THE PROLETARIAN REVOLUTION

1. Foundations of the Marxian Theory of the Proletarian Revolution

A. Laws of Social Development

My investigation led to the result that legal relations such as forms of state are to be grasped neither from themselves nor from the so-called general development of the human mind, but rather have their roots in the material conditions of life, the sum total of which Hegel, in accordance with the procedure of the Englishmen and Frenchmen of the eighteenth century, includes together under the name of "civil society,"* but that the anatomy of civil society is to be sought in political economy. The investigation of the latter, which I began in Paris, I continued at Brussels, whither I had emigrated in consequence of an expulsion order of M. Guizot. The general result at which I arrived and which, once won, served as a guiding thread for my studies, can be briefly formulated as follows: In the social production which men carry on they enter into definite relations that are indispensable and independent of their will; these relations of production correspond to a definite stage of development of their material powers of production. The sum total of these relations of production constitutes the economic structure of society – the real foundation, on which rises a legal and political superstructure and to which correspond definite forms of social consciousness. The mode of production in material life determines the general character of the social, political and spiritual processes of life. It is not the consciousness of men that determines their existence, but, on the contrary, their social existence determines their consciousness. At a certain stage of their development, the material forces of production in society come in conflict with the existing relations of production, or – what is but a legal expression for the same thing –

---

* In German *bürgerlich* means both "civil" and "bourgeois." Hegel gives the name of "civil society" to the totality of economic relations (proprietary, cultural, every-day relationships) in contraposition to the state. – *Ed.*

with the property relations within which they have been at work before. From forms of development of the forces of production these relations turn into their fetters. Then comes the period of social revolution. With the change of the economic foundation the entire immense superstructure is more or less rapidly transformed. In considering such transformations a distinction should always be made between the material transformation of the economic conditions of production which can be determined with the precision of natural science, and the legal, political, religious, esthetic or philosophic – in short, ideological forms in which men become conscious of this conflict and fight it out. Just as our opinion of an individual is not based on what he thinks of himself, so can we not judge of such a period of transformation by its own consciousness; on the contrary, this consciousness must rather be explained from the contradictions of material life, from the existing conflict between the social forces of production and the relations of production. No social order ever disappears before all the productive forces for which there is room in it have been developed; and new higher relations of production never appear before the material conditions of their existence have matured in the womb of the old society. Therefore, mankind always takes up only such problems as it can solve; since, looking at the matter more closely, we will always find that the problem itself arises only when the material conditions necessary for its solution already exist or are at least in the process of formation. In broad outlines we can designate the Asiatic, the ancient, the feudal, and the modern bourgeois methods of production as so many epochs in the progress of the economic formation of society. The bourgeois relations of production are the last antagonistic form of the social process of production – antagonistic not in the sense of individual antagonism, but of one arising from conditions surrounding the life of individuals in society; at the same time the productive forces developing in the womb of bourgeois society create the material conditions for the solution of that antagonism. This social formation constitutes, therefore, the closing chapter of the prehistoric stage of human society.

Karl Marx, Preface to *Contribution to the Critique of Political Economy.*

B. Development of the Contradictions of Capitalism, and Inevitability of its Downfall

As soon as this process of transformation has sufficiently decomposed the old society from top to bottom, as soon as the laborers are turned into proletarians, their means of labor into capital, as soon as the capitalist mode of production stands on its own feet, then the further socialization of labor and further transformation of the land and other means of production into socially exploited and, therefore, common means of production, as well as the further expropriation of private proprietors, takes a new form. That which is now to be expropriated is no longer the laborer working for himself, but the capitalist exploiting many laborers.

This expropriation is accomplished by the action of the immanent laws of capitalistic production itself, by the centralization of capital. One capitalist always kills many. Hand in hand with this centralization, or this expropriation of many capitalists by few, develop, on an ever-extending scale, the cooperative form of the labor-process, the conscious technical application of science, the methodical cultivation of the soil, the transformation of the instruments of labor into instruments of labor only usable in common, the economizing of all means of production by their use as the means of production of combined, socialized labor, the entanglement of all peoples in the net of the world-market, and with this, the international character of the capitalistic regime. Along with the constantly diminishing number of the magnates of capital, who usurp and monopolize all advantages of this process of transformation, grows the mass of misery, oppression, slavery, degradation, exploitation; but with this too grows the revolt of the working class, a class always increasing in numbers, and disciplined, united, organized by the very mechanism of the process of capitalist production itself. The monopoly of capital becomes a fetter upon the mode of production, which has sprung up and flourished along with and under it. Centralization of the means of production and socialization of labor at last reach a point where they become incompatible with their capitalist integument. This integument is burst asunder. The knell of capitalist private property sounds. The expropriators are expropriated.

The capitalist mode of appropriation, the result of the capitalist mode of production, produces capitalist private property. This is the first negation of individual private property, as founded on the labor of the proprietor. But capitalist production begets, with the inexorability of a law of nature, its own negation. It is the negation of negation. This does not reestablish private property for the producer, but gives him individual property based on the acquisitions of the capitalist era: *i.e.,* on cooperation and the possession in common of the land and of the means of production.

The transformation of scattered private property, arising from individual labor, into capitalist private property is, naturally, a process incomparably more protracted, violent and difficult than the transformation of capitalistic private property, already practically resting on socialized production, into socialized property. In the former case, we had the expropriation of the mass of the people by a few usurpers; in the latter, we have the expropriation of a few usurpers by the mass of the people.

Karl Marx, "Historical Tendency of Capitalist Accumulation," *Capital,* Vol. I.

C. Marx and Engels on the Inevitability of the Socialist Revolution and the Historical Role of the Proletariat

Modern bourgeois society with its relations of production, of exchange and of property, a society that has conjured up such gigantic means of production and of exchange, is like the sorcerer who is no longer able to control the powers of the nether world whom he has called up by his spells. For many a decade past the history of industry and commerce is but the history of the revolt of modern productive forces against modern conditions of production, against the property relations that are the conditions for the existence of the bourgeoisie and of its rule. It is enough to mention the commercial crises that by their periodical return put the existence of the entire bourgeois society on its trial, each time more threateningly. In these crises a great part not only of the existing products, but also of the previously created productive forces, are periodically destroyed. In these crises there breaks out an epidemic that, in all earlier epochs, would have seemed an absurdity – the epidemic of over-production. Society suddenly finds itself put back into a state of momentary barbarism; it appears as if a famine, a universal war of devastation had cut off the supply of every means of subsistence; industry and commerce seem to be destroyed. And why? Because there is too much civilization, too much means of subsistence, too much industry, too much commerce. The productive forces at the disposal of society no longer tend to further the development of the conditions of bourgeois property; on the contrary, they have become too powerful for these conditions, by which they are fettered, and so soon as they overcome these fetters, they bring disorder into the whole of bourgeois society, endanger the existence of bourgeois property. The conditions of bourgeois society are too narrow to comprise the wealth created by them. And how does the bourgeoisie get over these crises? On the one hand by enforced destruction of a mass of productive forces; on the other, by the conquest of new markets, and by the more thorough exploitation of the old ones. That is to say, by paving the way for more extensive and more destructive crises, and by diminishing the means whereby crises are prevented.

The weapons with which the bourgeoisie felled feudalism to the ground are now turned against the bourgeoisie itself.

But not only has the bourgeoisie forged the weapons that bring death to itself; it has also called into existence the men who are to wield those weapons – the modern working class – the proletarians.

In proportion as the bourgeoisie, *i.e.,* capital, is developed, in the same proportion is the proletariat, the modern working class, developed – a class of laborers, who live only so long as they find work, and who find work only so long as their labor increases capital. These laborers, who must sell themselves piecemeal, are a commodity, like every other article of commerce, and are consequently exposed to all the vicissitudes of competition, to all the fluctuations of the market.

Owing to the extensive use of machinery and to division of labor, the work of the proletarians has lost all individual character, and, consequently, all charm for the workman. He becomes an appendage of the machine, and it is only the most simple, most monotonous, and most easily acquired knack, that is required of him. Hence the cost of production of a workman is restricted, almost entirely, to the means of subsistence that he requires for his maintenance, and for the propagation of his race. But the price of a commodity, and therefore also of labor, is equal to its cost of production. In proportion, therefore, as the repulsiveness of the work increases, the wage decreases. Nay more, in proportion as the use of machinery and division of labor increases, in the same proportion the burden of toil also increases, whether by prolongation of the working hours, by increase of the work exacted in a given time, or

11

by increased speed of the machinery, etc.

Modern industry has converted the little workshop of the patriarchal master into the great factory of the industrial capitalist. Masses of laborers, crowded into the factory, are organized like soldiers. As privates of the industrial army they are placed under the command of a perfect hierarchy of officers and sergeants. Not only are they slaves of the bourgeois class, and of the bourgeois state; they are daily and hourly enslaved by the machine, by the over-looker, and, above all, by the individual bourgeois manufacturer himself. The more openly this despotism proclaims gain to be its end and aim, the more petty, the more hateful and the more embittering it is.

The less the skill and exertion of strength implied in manual labor, in other words, the more modern industry becomes developed, the more is the labor of men superseded by that of women. Differences of age and sex have no longer any distinctive social validity for the working class. All are instruments of labor, more or less expensive to use, according to their age and sex.

No sooner is the exploitation of the laborer by the manufacturer so far at an end that he receives his wages in cash, than he is set upon by the other portions of the bourgeoisie, the landlord, the shopkeeper, the pawnbroker, etc.

The lower strata of the middle class – the small trades-people, shopkeepers, and retired tradesmen generally, the handicraftsmen and peasants – all these sink gradually into the proletariat, partly because their diminutive capital does not suffice for the scale on which modern industry is carried on, and is swamped in the competition with the large capitalists, partly because their specialized skill is rendered worthless by new methods of production. Thus the proletariat is recruited from all classes of the population.

The proletariat goes through various stages of development. With its birth begins its struggle with the bourgeoisie. At first the contest is carried on by individual laborers, then by the work people of a factory, then by the operatives of one trade, in one locality, against the individual bourgeois who directly exploits them. They direct their attacks not against the bourgeois conditions of production, but against the instruments of production themselves; they destroy imported wares that compete with their labor, they smash to pieces machinery, they set factories ablaze, they seek to restore by force the vanished status of the workman of the Middle Ages.

At this stage the laborers still form an incoherent mass scattered over the whole country, and broken up by their mutual competition. If anywhere they unite to form more compact bodies, this is not yet the consequence of their own active union, but of the union of the bourgeoisie, which class, in order to attain its own political ends, is compelled to set the whole proletariat in motion, and is moreover yet, for a time, able to do so. At this stage, therefore, the proletarians do not fight their enemies, but the enemies of their enemies, the remnants of absolute monarchy, the landowners, the non-industrial bourgeois, the petty bourgeoisie. Thus the whole historical movement is concentrated in the hands of the bourgeoisie; every victory so obtained is a victory for the bourgeoisie.

But with the development of industry the proletariat not only increases in number; it becomes concentrated in greater masses, its strength grows, and it feels that strength more. The various interests and conditions of life within the ranks of the proletariat are more and more equalized, in proportion as machinery obliterates all distinctions of labor, and nearly everywhere reduces wages to the same low level. The growing competition among the bourgeois, and the resulting commercial crisis, make the wages of the workers ever more fluctuating. The unceasing improvement of machinery, ever more rapidly developing, makes their livelihood more and more precarious; the collisions between individual workmen and individual bourgeois take more and more the character of collisions between two classes. Thereupon the workers begin to form combinations (trade unions) against the bourgeois; they club together in order to keep up the rate of wages; they found permanent associations in order to make provision beforehand for these occasional revolts. Here and there the contest breaks out into riots.

Now and then the workers are victorious, but only for a time. The real fruit of their battles lies, not in the immediate result, but in the ever-expanding union of the workers. This union is helped on by the improved means of communication that are created by modern industry, and that place the workers of different localities in contact with one another. It was just this contact that was needed to centralize the numerous local struggles, all of the same character, into one national struggle between classes. But every class struggle is a political struggle. And that union, to attain which the burghers of the Middle Ages, with their miserable highways, required centuries, the modern proletarians, thanks to railways, achieve in a few years.

This organization of the proletarians into a class, and consequently into a political party, is continually being upset again by the competition between the workers themselves. But it ever rises up again, stronger, firmer, mightier. It compels legislative recognition of particular interests of the workers, by taking advantage of the divisions among the bourgeoisie itself. Thus the ten-hour bill in England was carried.

Altogether, collisions between the classes of the old society further in many ways the course of development of the proletariat. The bourgeoisie finds itself involved in a constant battle. At first with the aristocracy; later on, with those portions of the bourgeoisie itself, whose interests have become antagonistic to the progress of industry; at all times with the bourgeoisie of foreign countries. In all these battles it sees itself compelled to appeal to the proletariat, to ask for its help, and thus, to drag it into the political arena. The bourgeoisie itself, therefore, supplies the proletariat with its own elements of political and general education; in other words, it furnishes the proletariat with weapons for fighting the bourgeoisie.

Further, as we have already seen, entire sections of the ruling classes are, by the advance of industry, precipitated into the proletariat, or are at least threatened in their conditions of existence. These also supply the proletariat with fresh elements of enlightenment and progress.

Finally, in times when the class struggle nears the decisive hour, the process of dissolution going on within the ruling class, in fact within the whole range of old society, assumes such a violent, glaring character, that a small section of the ruling class cuts itself adrift, and joins the revolutionary class, the class that holds the future in its hands. Just as, therefore, at an earlier period, a section of the nobility went over to the bourgeoisie, so now a portion of the bourgeoisie goes over to the proletariat, and in particular, a portion of the bourgeois ideologists, who have raised themselves to the level of comprehending theoretically the historical movement as a whole.

Of all the classes that stand face to face with the bourgeoisie today, the proletariat alone is a really revolutionary class. The other classes decay and finally disappear in the face of modern industry; the proletariat is its special and essential product.

The lower middle class, the small manufacturer, the shopkeeper, the artisan, the peasant, all these fight against the bourgeoisie, to save from extinction their existence as fractions of the middle class. They are therefore not revolutionary, but conservative. Nay more, they are reactionary, for they try to roll back the wheel of history. If by chance they are revolutionary, they are so only in view of their impending transfer into the proletariat; they thus defend not their present, but their future interests; they desert their own standpoint to place themselves at that of the proletariat.

The "dangerous class," the social scum, that passively rotting mass thrown off by the lowest layers of old society, may, here and there, be swept into the movement by a proletarian revolution; its conditions of life, however, prepare it far more for the part of a bribed tool of reactionary intrigue.

In the conditions of the proletariat, those of old society at large are already virtually swamped. The proletarian is without property; his relation to his wife and children has no longer anything in common with the bourgeois family relations; modern industrial labor, modern subjection to capital, the same in England as in France, in America as in Germany, has stripped him of every trace of national character. Law, morality, religion, are to him so many bourgeois prejudices, behind which lurk in ambush just as many bourgeois interests.

All the preceding classes that got the upper hand, sought to fortify their already acquired status by subjecting society at large to their conditions of appropriation. The proletarians cannot become masters of the productive forces of society, except by abolishing their own previous mode of appropriation. They have nothing of their own to secure and to fortify; their mission is to destroy all previous securities for, and insurances of, individual property.

All previous historical movements were movements of minorities, or in the interest of minorities. The proletarian movement is the self-conscious, independent movement of the immense majority, in the interest of the immense majority. The proletariat, the lowest stratum of our present society, cannot stir, cannot raise itself up, without the whole superincumbent strata of official society being sprung into the air.

Though not in substance, yet in form, the struggle of the proletariat with the bourgeoisie is at first a national struggle. The proletariat of each country must, of course, first of all settle matters with its own bourgeoisie.

In depicting the most general phases of the development of the proletariat, we traced the more or less veiled civil war, raging within existing society, up to the point where that war breaks out into open revolution, and where the violent overthrow of the bourgeoisie lays the foundation for the sway of the proletariat.

Hitherto, every form of society has been based, as we have already seen, on the antagonism of oppressing and oppressed classes. But in order to oppress a class, certain conditions must be assured to it under which it can, at least, continue its slavish existence. The serf, in the period of serfdom, raised himself to membership in the commune, just as the petty bourgeois, under the yoke of feudal absolutism, managed to develop into a bourgeois. The modern laborer, on the contrary, instead of rising with the progress of industry, sinks deeper and deeper below the conditions of existence of his own class. He becomes a pauper, and pauperism develops more rapidly than population and wealth. And here it becomes evident, that the bourgeoisie is unfit any longer to be the ruling class in society, and to impose its conditions of existence upon society as an over-riding law. It is unfit to rule because it is incompetent to assure an existence to its slave within his slavery, because it cannot help letting him sink into such a state, that it has to feed him, instead of being fed by him. Society can no longer live under this bourgeoisie, in other words, its existence is no longer compatible with society.

The essential condition for the existence and for the sway of the bourgeois class, is the formation and augmentation of capital; the condition for capital is wage-labor. Wage-labor rests exclusively on competition between the laborers. The advance of industry, whose involuntary promoter is the bourgeoisie, replaces the isolation of the laborers, due to competition, by their revolutionary combination, due to association. The development of modern industry, therefore, cuts from under its feet the very foundation on which the bourgeoisie produces and appropriates products. What the bourgeoisie therefore produces, above all, are its own grave-diggers. Its fall and the victory of the proletariat are equally inevitable.

Karl Marx and Frederick Engels, *Communist Manifesto,* Chap. I.

2. Leninist Theory of Imperialism as the Last Stage of Capitalism and the Eve of the Proletarian Revolution

A. Stalin on the Leninist Theory of Imperialism

The Leninist theory of the proletarian revolution is based on three fundamental theses.

First Thesis: The domination of finance capital in the advanced capitalist countries, the issue of stocks and bonds as the principal operation of finance capital; the export of capital to the sources of raw materials, which is one of the bases of imperialism; the omnipotence of a financial oligarchy, a consequence of the domination of finance capital – all these reveal the crudely parasitic character of monopolist capitalism, make the yoke of the capitalist trusts and syndicates a hundred times more burdensome, increase the growth of the indignation of the working class against the foundation of capitalism and drive the masses to the proletarian revolution as their only means of escape. (Lenin, *Imperialism, the Highest Stage of Capitalism.*)

Hence the first conclusion that is to be drawn: an intensification of the revolutionary crisis in the capitalist countries and the growth of the elements of an explosion on the internal, proletarian front in the "mother countries."

Second Thesis: The growth of the export of capital to the colonies and dependent countries, the extension of "spheres of influence" and colonial possessions to the extent of seizing all the territory of the globe, the transformation of capitalism into a *world system* of financial bondage and of the colonial oppression of the vast majority of mankind by a handful of "advanced" countries – these factors have, on the one hand, converted the several national economic systems and national territories into links in a single chain called world economy and, on the other hand, have divided the population of the world into two camps: a handful of "advanced" capitalist countries which exploit and oppress vast colonies and dependencies, and the immense majority of the colonial and dependent countries, compelled to fight to liberate themselves from the imperialist yoke. (*Imperialism, the Highest Stage of Capitalism.*)

Hence the second conclusion to be drawn: an intensification of the revolutionary crisis in the colonial countries and an accumulation of the elements of discontent with imperialism on the external front, the colonial front.

Third Thesis: The monopolistic possession of "spheres of influence" and colonies, the uneven development of the different capitalist countries which leads to a bitter struggle for the re-division of the world between the countries which have already seized the territories of the globe, and those countries which want to receive their "share"; imperialist wars, the only method of restoring the disturbed "equilibrium" – all these lead to the reenforcement of the third front, the inter-capitalist front – which weakens imperialism and facilitates the union of the first two fronts against imperialism – the front of the revolutionary proletariat and that of colonial emancipation. (*Ibid.*)

Hence the third conclusion: the inevitability of wars under imperialism and the inevitability of a coalition between the proletarian revolution in Europe and the colonial revolution in the East, thus forming a united world front of the revolution as against the world front of imperialism.

Lenin combines all these conclusions into the general conclusion that "imperialism is the eve of the Socialist Revolution."

Joseph Stalin, *Foundations of Leninism,* Chap. III, Section 3

B. Imperialism as Moribund Capitalism – the Eve of the Proletarian Revolution

Imperialism is a particular historic stage of capitalism. Its special character is three-fold: imperialism is (1) monopoly capitalism; (2) parasitic, or decaying capitalism; (3) moribund capitalism. The substitution of monopoly for free competition is the fundamental economic feature, the *quintessence* of imperialism. Monopoly manifests itself in five main forms: (1) cartels, syndicates and trusts, the concentration of production having reached the stage which gives rise to these monopolistic combinations of capitalists; (2) the monopolistic position of big banks: three to five gigantic banks manipulate the whole economic life of America, France, Germany; (3) usurpation of the sources of *raw material* by the trusts and the financial oligarchy (finance capital is monopolistic industrial capital merged with bank capital); (4) the (economic) partition of the world among the international cartels has begun. The international cartels which dominate the *whole* world market, dividing it "amicably" among themselves – until war brings about a *re-distribution* – already number over *one hundred!* The export of capital, a specifically characteristic phenomenon distinct from export of commodities under non-monopoly capitalism, is closely bound up with the economic and territorial-political partition of the world; (5) the territorial partition of the world (colonies) is *completed.*

Imperialism, as the highest stage of capitalism in America and Europe, and later in Asia, fully developed in the period 1898-1914: The Spanish-American War (1898), the Anglo-Boer War (1900-02), the Russo-Japanese War (1904-05) and the economic crisis in Europe in 1900 are the principal historic landmarks in the new era of world history.

The fact that imperialism is parasitic or decaying manifests itself first of all in the tendency to decay which distinguishes *all* monopoly under the system of private ownership of the means of production. The difference between the republican-democratic and the monarchist-reactionary imperialist bourgeoisie is obliterated precisely because both are rotting alive (which by no means prevents the astonishingly rapid development of capitalism in individual branches of industry, individual countries, individual periods). Secondly, the decay of capitalism manifests itself in the creation of a huge stratum of *rentiers,* capitalists who live by clipping coupons. In each of the four advanced imperialist countries, England, North America, France and Germany, capital in securities amounts to one hundred to one hundred fifty *billion* francs, from which each country derives an annual income of no less than five to eight billions. Thirdly, capital export is parasitism multiplied. Fourthly, "finance capital tends towards domination, not towards freedom." Political reaction *all along the line* is a concomitant of imperialism. Corruption, bribery in gigantic proportions, Panamas of all kinds. Fifthly, exploitation of oppressed nations, inseparably connected with annexations, especially the exploitation of colonies by a handful of "Great Powers," transforms the "civilized" world more and more into a parasite on the body of hundreds of millions of uncivilized peoples. The Roman proletarian lived at the expense of society. Modern society lives at the expense of the modern proletariat. Marx particularly emphasized this profound observation of Sismondi. Imperialism changes the situation somewhat. A privileged upper stratum of the proletariat in the imperialist countries lives partly at the expense of the hundreds of millions of uncivilized peoples.

It is clear why imperialism is *moribund* capitalism, the *transition* to socialism: monopoly growing *out* of capitalism is already the dying out of capitalism, the beginning of its transition to socialism. The tremendous *socialization* of labor by imperialism (what the apologetic bourgeois economists call "interlocking") signifies the same thing.

V. I. Lenin, "Imperialism and the Split in the Socialist Movement," *Collected Works,* Russian edition, Vol. XIX.

C. Maturity of the Material Preconditions for the Transition to Socialism in the Epoch of Imperialism

Competition is transformed into monopoly. The result is an immense progress in the socialization of production. The process of technical invention and improvement, in particular, is becoming socialized.

This is no longer the old type of free competition between manufacturers, scattered and uninformed about one another, and producing for an unknown market. Concentration has reached the point where it is possible to make an approximate survey of all sources of raw material (for example, the iron ore deposits) of a country, and even, as we shall see, of several countries, or of the whole world. Not only are such surveys made, but these sources are seized by gigantic monopolist associations. An approximate estimate of the capacity of the market is also made, and these associations "divide" it up among themselves by contractual agreement. Skilled labor is monopolized, the best engineers are engaged; the means of transportation – railways in America, steamship companies in Europe and America – are seized. Capitalism, in its imperialist stage, arrives at the threshold of the most universal socialization of production. It drags, as it were, the capitalists, against their will and understanding, into some new social order, which is transitional, leading from complete freedom of competition to complete socialization.

V. I. Lenin, *Imperialism, the Highest Stage of Capitalism,* Little Lenin Library, Vol. 15, pp. 24-25.

Justice by itself, the mere feelings of the indignant exploited masses, would never have led them on the right road to Socialism. But when, thanks to capitalism, there grew up the material apparatus of big banks, syndicates, railways, and so on; when the very rich experience of the advanced countries has amassed a hoard of marvelous technical knowledge, the application of which capitalism is now *hindering;* when the class-conscious workers have formed a party of a quarter of a million members for the purpose of taking this apparatus into their hands in a planned fashion and setting it going with the support of all the laboring and exploited masses – when these conditions are present, then there is no force on earth which can prevent the Bolsheviks, *if only they do not allow themselves to be cowed* and are able to seize power, from retaining it until the victory of the world socialist revolution.

> V. I. Lenin, "Will the Bolsheviks Retain State Power?" *Collected Works,* Vol. XXI, Book 2, p. 51; also Little Lenin Library, Vol. 12, p. 42.

The imperialist war is –the eve of the Socialist revolution. And this is so not only because the war with its horrors is generating a proletarian uprising – no uprising will create Socialism if it has not ripened economically – but because state monopoly capitalism is the fullest *material* preparation for Socialism, is its *threshold,* is that rung on the historic ladder between which rung and the one called Socialism *there are no intermediate rungs.*

> V. I. Lenin, "The Threatening Catastrophe," *Collected Works,* Vol. XXI, Book 1, p. 212; also Little Lenin Library, Vol. 11, p. 38.

D. Imperialism, a Spasmodic Epoch Full of Catastrophes and Conflicts

There had been an epoch of a comparatively "peaceful" capitalism, when it had finally overcome feudalism in the advanced countries of Europe and was in a position to develop most – *comparatively* – tranquilly and smoothly, "peacefully" spreading over tremendous areas of still unoccupied lands, and of countries not yet finally drawn into the capitalist vortex. Of course, even in that epoch, marked approximately by the years 1871-1914, "peaceful" capitalism created conditions of life that were very, very far from being really peaceful both in the military and in a general class sense. For nine-tenths of the population of the advanced countries, for hundreds of millions of peoples in the colonies and in the backward countries this epoch was not one of "peace" but of oppression, tortures, horrors that were, perhaps, the more terrifying since they appeared to be "horrors without end." This epoch has gone never to return; it has been followed by an epoch, comparatively much more impetuous, spasmodic, full of catastrophes and conflicts, an epoch that to the toiling masses is no longer typified so much by horror without end as by an "end with horror."

It is highly important to bear in mind that this change was caused solely by the direct development, growth, continuation of the most deep-seated and fundamental tendencies of capitalism and commodity production in general. The growth of commodity exchange, the growth of large-scale production, are the fundamental tendencies observable for centuries throughout the whole world. At a certain stage in the development of exchange, at a certain stage in the growth of large-scale production, namely, at the stage that was reached approximately at the end of the nineteenth and the beginning of the twentieth centuries, commodity exchange had created such an internationalization of economic relations, and such an internationalization of capital, large-scale production became so vast that free competition began to be replaced by monopoly. The prevailing types were no longer enterprises freely competing inside the country and *through intercourse between countries,* but monopoly alliances of entrepreneurs, trusts. The typical "boss" of the world now became finance capital, a power that is peculiarly mobile and flexible, peculiarly intertwined at home and internationally, peculiarly devoid of individuality and divorced from the immediate processes of production, peculiarly easy to concentrate, a power that has already made peculiarly large strides on the road of concentration, so that literally several hundred billionaires and millionaires hold the fate of the whole world in their hands.

Reasoning theoretically and *in the abstract,* one may arrive at the conclusion reached by Kautsky (who likewise has parted ways with Marxism, but in a different manner), *viz.,* that the time is not far off when these magnates of capital will unite into one world trust which will replace the rivalries and the struggle of nationally-bound finance capital by an internationally united finance capital.* Such a conclusion, however, is just as abstract, simplified and incorrect as an analogous conclusion arrived at by our "Struveists" and

---

* Editor's Note: Here for instance is what Kautsky wrote in 1916: *"The present phase of imperialism need not be the last form in which capitalism will appear....* The development does not proceed in a straight line but dialectically, *i.e.,* through contradictions. Thus mercantilism engendered free trade and the latter engendered imperialism. *The possibility is not excluded that this will again be followed by a new era of capitalism* in conditions which will make possible a *league of states* such as that of Central Europe, on the basis of its members joining voluntarily and gladly, which would ensure its *enduring and beneficial functioning."* (Karl Kautsky: *The United States of Central Europe,* Stuttgart, 1916, p. 48.)

"Economists" of the nineties of the last century. The latter, proceeding from the progressive nature of capitalism, from its inevitability, from its final victory in Russia, at times made apologetic conclusions (worshiping capital, reconcilement to it, praising it instead of fighting it); at times non-political conclusions (*i.e.*, rejected politics, or denied the importance of politics, the probability of general political convulsions, etc., this being the favorite error of the "Economists") ; at times even outright "strike" conclusions (the "general strike" to them was the apotheosis of the strike movement; it was elevated to a position where other forms of the movement are forgotten or ignored; it was a *salto mortale* from capitalism to its destruction by strikes alone and nothing else). There are indications that the undisputed progressiveness of capitalism, compared with the semi-philistine "paradise" of free competition, and the inevitability of imperialism with its final victory over "peaceful" capital in the advanced countries of the world, may also at present lead to political and non-political errors and misadventures no less numerous or varied.

Particularly as regards Kautsky, his open break with Marxism has led him, not to reject or forget politics, nor to "skim" *over* the numerous and varied political conflicts, convulsions and transformations that particularly characterize the imperialist epoch; nor to become an apologist of imperialism, but to *dream about a "peaceful capitalism."* "Peaceful" capitalism has been replaced by unpeaceful, militant, catastrophic imperialism. This Kautsky is compelled to admit, for he admitted it as early as 1909 in a special work in which he drew sound conclusions as a Marxist for the last time. If it is thus impossible simply, directly, and bluntly to dream of going back from imperialism to "peaceful" capitalism, is it not possible to give those essentially petty-bourgeois dreams the appearance of innocent contemplations regarding "peaceful" "ultra-imperialism"? If the name of ultra-imperialism is given to an international unification of national (or, more correctly, state-bound) imperialisms which "would be able" to eliminate the conflicts that are particularly unpleasant, particularly alarming and disturbing to the petty bourgeois, such as wars, political convulsions, etc., then why not turn away from the present epoch of imperialism that has already arrived – the epoch that stares one in the face, that is full of all sorts of conflicts and catastrophes? Why not turn to innocent dreams of a comparatively peaceful, comparatively conflictless, comparatively noncatastrophic "ultra-imperialism"? And why not wave aside the "exacting" tasks posed by the epoch of imperialism that has arrived in Europe and dream that this epoch will perhaps soon be over, that perhaps it will be followed by a comparatively "peaceful" epoch of ultra-imperialism which demands no such "exacting" tactics? This is precisely what Kautsky says, that at any rate "such a new [ultra-imperialist] phase of capitalism is thinkable, but whether it can be realized – to answer this question we have not yet sufficient data." (*Neue Zeit,* April 30, 1915, p. 144.)

In this striving to brush aside the imperialism that is here and to pass in dreams to an epoch of "ultra-imperialism," of which we do not know whether it is realizable, there is not a grain of Marxism. In this structure Marxism is admitted for that "new phase of capitalism," for the *realizability* of which its inventor himself fails to vouch, while for the present, the existing phase of capitalism, he offers us not Marxism, but a petty-bourgeois and deeply reactionary endeavor to soften contradictions. There was a time when Kautsky *promised* to be a Marxist in the coming restless and catastrophic epoch, which he was compelled to foresee and quite definitely recognize when writing his work in 1909 about this coming epoch. Now, when it has become absolutely clear that that epoch has arrived, Kautsky again only *promises* to be a Marxist in the coming epoch of ultra-imperialism, of whose realizability he is not at all certain! In other words, we have any number of his promises to be a Marxist some time in a *future* epoch, not now, not under present conditions, not at this moment! For to-morrow we have Marxism on credit, Marxism as a promise. For to-day we have a petty-bourgeois, opportunist theory – and not only a theory – of softening contradictions. It is something like the internationalism for export so widespread "in our days" when ardent – ever so ardent! – internationalists and Marxists sympathize with every expression of internationalism – in the enemy's camp, anywhere, only not at home, not among their allies; sympathize with democracy as long as it remains a promise of their "allies"; sympathize with the "self-determination of nations," but *not* of those that are dependent upon a nation that has the honor of counting the sympathizer among its adherents – in a word, this is one of the thousand and one varieties of hypocrisy.

Can one, however, dispute that in the abstract a new phase of capitalism *after* imperialism, namely, a phase of ultra-imperialism, is "thinkable"? No. In the abstract one can think of such a phase. In practice, however, it means to become an opportunist who rejects the hard tasks of to-day for the sake of dreams about easy tasks of the future. Theoretically it means not to base oneself on the developments now going on in real life, to *detach* oneself from them in the name of dreams. There is no doubt that the development is going *in the direction* of a single world trust that will swallow up all enterprises and all states without exception. But the development in this direction is proceeding under such circumstances, with such a tempo, with such contradictions, conflicts, and convulsions – not only economic, but also political, national, etc., etc. – that *before* a single world trust will be reached, before the respective national finance capitals will have formed a world union of "ultra-imperialism," imperialism will inevitably explode, capitalism will turn into its opposite.

V. I. Lenin, Introduction to N. I. Bukharin's *Imperialism and World Economy.*

E. Imperialism and the Crash of Capitalism

Imperialism has greatly developed the productive forces of world capitalism. It has completed the preparation of all the material prerequisites for the socialist organization of society. By its wars it has demonstrated that the productive forces of world economy, which have outgrown the restricted boundaries of imperialist states, demand the organization of economy on a world, or international scale. Imperialism tries to remove this contradiction by hacking a road with fire and sword towards a single world state-capitalist trust, which is to organize the whole world economy. This sanguinary utopia is being extolled by the social-democratic ideologists as a peaceful method of newly "organized" capitalism. In reality, this utopia encounters insurmountable objective obstacles of such magnitude that capitalism must inevitably fall beneath the weight of its own contradictions. The law of uneven development of capitalism, which becomes intensified in the epoch of imperialism, renders firm and durable international combinations of imperialist powers impossible. On the other hand, imperialist wars, which are developing into world wars, and by which the law of the centralization of capitalism strives to reach its world limit – a single world trust – are accompanied by so much destruction and place such burdens upon the shoulders of the working class and of the millions of colonial proletarians and peasants, that capitalism must inevitably perish beneath the blows of the proletarian revolution long before this goal is reached.

Being the highest phase of capitalist development, developing the productive forces of world economy to enormous dimensions, refashioning the whole world after its own image, imperialism draws within the orbit of finance capitalist exploitation all colonies, all races and all nations. At the same time, however, the monopolist form of capital increasingly develops the elements of parasitical degeneration, decay and decline of capitalism. In destroying, to some extent, the driving force of competition, by conducting a policy of cartel prices, and by having undivided mastery of the market, monopoly capital reveals a tendency to retard the further development of the forces of production. In squeezing enormous sums of surplus profits out of the millions of colonial workers and peasants and in accumulating colossal incomes from this exploitation, imperialism is creating a type of decaying and parasitically degenerate rentier class, as well as whole strata of parasites who live by clipping coupons. In completing the process of creating the material prerequisites for socialism (the concentration of means of production, the enormous socialization of labor, the growth of labor organizations), the epoch of imperialism intensifies the antagonisms among the "Great Powers" and gives rise to wars which cause the break-up of single world economy. Imperialism is therefore moribund and decaying capitalism. It is the final stage of development of the capitalist system. It is the threshold of world social revolution.

Hence, international proletarian revolution logically emerges out of the conditions of development of capitalism generally, and out of its imperialist phase in particular. The capitalist system as a whole is approaching its final collapse.

The dictatorship of finance capital is perishing to give way to the dictatorship of the proletariat.

Program of the Communist International, Part I, Section 4.

F. General Crisis of Capitalism

The imperialist struggle among the largest capitalist states for the redistribution of the globe led to the first imperialist world war (1914-1918). This war shook the whole system of world capitalism and marked the beginning of the period of its general crisis. It bent to its service the entire national economy of the belligerent countries, thus creating the mailed fist of state capitalism; it increased unproductive expenditures to enormous dimensions, destroyed enormous quantities of the means of production and human labor power, ruined large masses of the population and imposed incalculable burdens upon the industrial workers, the peasants and the colonial peoples. It inevitably led to the intensification of the class struggle, which grew into open, revolutionary mass action and civil war. The imperialist front was broken at its weakest link, in tsarist Russia. The February revolution of 1917 overthrew the domination of the autocracy of the big landowning class. The October revolution overthrew the rule of the bourgeoisie. This victorious proletarian revolution expropriated the expropriators, took the means of production from the landlords and the capitalists, and for the first time in human history set up and consolidated the dictatorship of the proletariat in an enormous country, brought into being a new, Soviet type of state and laid the foundations for the international proletarian revolution.

The powerful shock to which the whole of world capitalism was subjected, the sharpening of the class struggle and the direct influence of the October proletarian revolution gave rise to a series of revolutions and revolutionary actions on the continent of Europe as well as in the colonial and semi-colonial countries: January, 1918, the proletarian revolution in Finland; August, 1918, the so-called "rice riots" in Japan; November, 1918, the revolutions in Austria and Germany, which overthrew the semi-feudal monarchist regime; March, 1919, the proletarian revolution in Hungary and the uprising in Korea; April, 1919, the Soviet Government in Bavaria; January, 1920, the bourgeois-national revolution in Turkey; September, 1920, the seizure of the factories by the workers in Italy; March, 1921, the rising of the advanced workers of Germany; September, 1923, the uprising in Bulgaria; Autumn, 1923, the revolutionary crisis in Germany; December, 1924, the uprising in Esthonia; April, 1923, the uprising in Morocco; August, 1925, uprising in Syria; May, 1926, the general strike in England; July, 1927, the proletarian uprising in Vienna. These events, as well as events like the uprising in Indonesia, the deep ferment in India, the great Chinese revolution, which shook the whole Asiatic continent, are links in one and the same international revolutionary chain, constituent parts of the profound general crisis of capitalism. This international revolutionary process embraced the immediate struggle for the dictatorship of the proletariat, as well as national wars of liberation and colonial uprisings against imperialism, which go together with the agrarian mass movement of millions of peasants. Thus, an enormous mass of humanity was swept into the revolutionary torrent. World history entered a new phase of development – a phase of prolonged general crisis of the capitalist system. In this process, the unity of world economy found expression in the international character of the revolution, while the uneven development of its separate parts was expressed in the different times of the outbreak of revolution in the different countries.

The first attempts at revolutionary overthrow, which sprang from the acute crisis of capitalism (1918-1921) ended in the victory and consolidation of the dictatorship of the proletariat in the U.S.S.R. and in the defeat of the proletariat in a number of other countries. These defeats were primarily due to the treacherous tactics of the social democratic and reformist trade union leaders, but they were also due to the fact that the majority of the working class had not yet accepted the lead of the Communists and that in a number of important countries Communist parties had not yet been established at all. As a result of these defeats, which created the opportunity for intensifying the exploitation of the mass of the proletariat and the colonial peoples, and for severely depressing their standard of living, the bourgeoisie was able to achieve a partial stabilization of capitalist relations.

Program of the Communist International, Part II, Section I.

The present economic crisis is developing on the basis of the *general crisis* of capitalism, which began during the period of the imperialist war, undermined the foundations of capitalism and paved the way for the present economic crisis.

What does this mean?

It means first of all that the imperialist war and its aftermath have intensified the decay of capitalism and described its equilibrium, that we are now living in the epoch of wars and revolutions; that capitalism no longer represents the *sole* and *all-embracing* system of world economy, that side by side with the *capitalist* system of economy there exists the *socialist* system, which is growing, which is flourishing, which is resisting the capitalist system, and which by the very fact of its existence is demonstrating the rottenness of capitalism and shaking its foundations.

It means, furthermore, that the imperialist war and the victory of the revolution in the U.S.S.R. have shaken the foundations of imperialism *in the colonial and dependent* countries, that the prestige of imperialism in these countries has already been undermined, that it is no longer capable of governing in the old way in these countries.

It means, further, that during the war and after it, a young, native capitalism appeared and grew up in the colonial and dependent countries, which competes successfully in the markets with the old capitalist countries, sharpening and complicating the struggle for markets.

It means, finally, that the war has left to the majority of the capitalist countries a painful heritage in the shape of *chronic underemployment of factories* and *armies of unemployed running into millions,* which, moreover, have been transformed from reserve into *permanent* armies of unemployed. This created a mass of difficulties for capitalism even before the present economic crisis, and must still further complicate matters during the crisis.

Such are the circumstances which aggravate and sharpen the world crisis.

It must be admitted that the present economic crisis is the most serious and profound world economic crisis that has ever occurred.

Joseph Stalin, *Leninism,* Vol. II, pp. 254-55.

G. Three Periods of Post-War Crisis

1. After the first world imperialist war, the international labor movement passed through a whole series of historical phases of development, expressing various phases of the general crisis of the capitalist system.

The *first* period was the period of extremely acute crisis of the capitalist system, and of direct revolutionary action on the part of the proletariat. This period reached its apex of development in 1921 and was terminated on the one hand by the victory of the U.S.S.R. over the forces of foreign intervention and internal counter-revolution, by the consolidation of the proletarian dictatorship and the organization of the Communist International. On the other hand it ended with a series of severe defeats for the West European proletariat and the beginning of the general capitalist offensive. The final link in the chain of events in this period was the defeat of the German proletariat in 1923.

This defeat marked the starting point of the *second* period, a period of a gradually forming partial stabilization of the capitalist system, of the "restoration" process of capitalist economy, of the development and expansion of the capitalist offensive and of the continuation of the defensive battles fought by the proletarian army weakened by severe defeats. On the other hand this period was a period of rapid restoration in the U.S.S.R., of extremely important successes in the work of building up Socialism and of the growth of the political influence of the Communist parties over the broad masses of the proletariat.

Finally, the *third* period which, in the main, is the period in which capitalist economy is exceeding the pre-war level and in which the economy of the U.S.S.R. is also almost simultaneously exceeding that level (the beginning of the "reconstruction period," so-called, the further growth of the socialist forms of economy on the basis of a new technique). For the capitalist system, this is the period of rapid development of technique and accelerated growth of cartels and trusts, of tendencies towards State capitalism, while, at the same time, it is a period of intense development of the contradictions of world economy moving in forms determined by the whole of the preceding process of the general crisis of capitalism (contraction of markets, the U.S.S.R., colonial movements, growth of the internal contradictions of imperialism). This third period, in which the contradiction between the growth of the productive forces and the contraction of markets becomes particularly accentuated, inevitably gives rise to a fresh series of imperialist wars: – of wars among the imperialist states themselves; of wars of the imperialist states against the U.S.S.R.; of wars of national liberation against imperialism and imperialist intervention and of gigantic class battles. The intensification of all *international* antagonisms (antagonisms between the capitalist states and the U.S.S.R., the military occupation of Northern China as the beginning of the partition of China and the struggles among the imperialists, etc.), the intensification of the *internal* antagonisms in the capitalist countries (the swing to the Left of the masses of the working class, growing acuteness of the class struggle), and the unleashing of *colonial movements* (China, India, Egypt, and Syria), which are taking place in this period, inevitably lead, – through the further development of the contradictions of capitalist stabilization, – to capitalist stabilization becoming still more precarious and to the severe intensification of the general crisis of capitalism.

Theses of the Sixth Congress of the Communist International, "The International Situation and the Tasks of the Communist International," *International Press Correspondence,* No. 83, 1928.

3. Motive Forces and Reserves of the World Socialist Revolution and the Role of the Party

A. Socialist Revolution – the Epoch Uniting Civil War of the Proletariat in the Advanced Countries with Numerous Democratic and Revolutionary Movements in the Backward Countries

The social revolution cannot be the united action of the proletarians of *all* countries, for the simple reason that the majority of the countries, and the majority of the inhabitants of the globe, have so far not even reached the capitalist stage of development or are only at the beginning of that stage.... The advanced countries of Western Europe and North America *alone* are ripe for socialism, and in Engels' letter to Kautsky (*Sbornik Sotsial-Demokrata*) P. Kievsky[*] may find a concrete illustration of the real, and not merely promised *"idea,"* that to dream of the "united action" of the proletarians of *all* countries means to postpone socialism to the Greek kalends, *i.e.,* forever.

Socialism will be achieved by the united action of the proletarians – not of all countries but of a minority of countries – the ones that have reached the stage of development of *advanced* capitalism. P. Kievsky's failure to understand this point is the cause of his error. In *those* advanced countries (England, France, Germany, etc.) the national problem was solved long ago; national unity has long outlived its purpose; *objectively,* there are no "national tasks" to be fulfilled. Hence, only in those countries is it possible *now* to "blow up" national unity, and establish class unity.

In the *undeveloped* countries, which we placed in a special category, namely, the whole of Eastern Europe and all the colonial and semi-colonial countries, the situation is entirely different. In those countries, as a general rule, we *still* have oppressed and capitalisti-

---

[*] Kievsky – pseudonym of Pyatakov whose article Lenin answers in the work from which this passage is taken. – *Ed.*

cally undeveloped nations. These nations still have *objectively* national tasks to fulfill, namely, *democratic* tasks, the tasks of *throwing off foreign oppression.*

...The victorious proletariat will reorganize the countries in which it has achieved victory. This cannot be done all at once; nor indeed is it possible, to "vanquish" the bourgeoisie all at once. We deliberately emphasized this in our theses, and P. Kievsky again failed to stop and think *why* we stressed this point in connection with the national problem.

The undeveloped and oppressed nations will not wait, they will not cease to live, they will not disappear, while the proletariat of the advanced countries is overthrowing the bourgeoisie and repelling its attempts at counter-revolution. If they take advantage even of such an imperialist bourgeois crisis as the war of 1915-16, which is only a minor crisis compared with a social revolution, to revolt (the colonies, Ireland), we can be quite sure that they will take advantage of the *great crisis* of civil war in the advanced countries to revolt all the more.

The social revolution cannot come about except as an epoch of civil war of the proletariat against the bourgeoisie in the advanced countries, combined with a *whole series* of democratic and revolutionary movements, including movements for national liberation, in the undeveloped, backward and oppressed nations.

Why? Because capitalism develops unevenly, and objective reality gives us highly developed capitalist nations side by side with a great many nations only slightly developed economically, or totally undeveloped. P. Kievsky has absolutely failed to study the *objective* conditions of social revolution from the point of view of the economic maturity of the various countries. Hence, his reproach about *our* "inventing" cases for applying self-determination falls not on our head, but on his own.

V. I. Lenin, "A Caricature of Marxism," Chapter V, *Collected Works,* Russian edition, Vol. XIX.

B. The Proletariat – the Only Consistent Revolutionary Class

...The factory worker is none other than the foremost representative of the whole of the exploited population, and in order that he may fulfill his function as a representative in the organized and sustained struggle, it is not at all necessary to try to tempt him with certain "perspectives"; all that is required for this purpose is that *his position be explained to him;* that the political and economic structure of the system which oppresses him, that the necessity and inevitability of class antagonisms under this system be explained to him. The position which the factory worker occupies in the general system of capitalist relationships makes him the sole fighter for the emancipation of the working class, because only the higher stage of development of capitalism, large-scale machine industry, creates the material conditions and the social forces that are necessary for this struggle. In all other places, where the forms of development of capitalism are low, these material conditions do not exist; production is broken up into thousands of tiny enterprises (and they do not cease to be fragmentary *enterprises* even under the most equalitarian forms of communal landownership), the exploited, in the majority of cases, still possess tiny enterprises and for that reason they attach themselves to the very bourgeois system which they should be fighting: this retards and hinders the development of the social forces that are capable of overthrowing capitalism. Fragmented, individual, petty exploitation binds the toilers to a particular place, disunites them, prevents them from appreciating their class solidarity, prevents them from uniting and from understanding that they are exploited not by this or that individual, but by the whole economic system. Large-scale capitalism, on the contrary, inevitably breaks all the worker's ties with the old society, with a particular locality and with a particular exploiter; it unties him, compels him to think and puts him in conditions which enable him to commence the organized struggle. It is on the working class that the Social-Democrats concentrate all their attention and all their activities. When the advanced representatives of this class will have mastered the ideas of scientific socialism, the idea of the historical role of the Russian worker, when these ideas become widespread and when durable organizations arise among the workers which will transform the present sporadic economic war of the workers into a conscious class struggle – then the Russian *workers* will rise at the head of all the democratic elements, overthrow absolutism and lead the *Russian proletariat* (side by side with the proletariat of *all countries*) *along the straight road of open political struggle towards the victorious communist revolution.*

V. I. Lenin, "What the 'Friends of the People' Are," *Selected Works,* Vol. I, pp. 453-455.

C. The Toiling Peasantry – the Reserve of the Proletariat in the Socialist Revolution

The masses of the rural toilers and exploited, whom the urban proletarian must lead into the struggle, or, at all events, win over to its side, are represented in all capitalist countries by the following classes:

First, the agricultural proletariat, wage workers (by the year, season or day), who obtain their livelihood by working for wages in capitalist agricultural enterprises. The organization of this class (political, military, trade union, cooperative, cultural and educational, etc.) independently and separately from other groups of the rural population, conducting intense propaganda and agitation among this class, winning it over to the side of the Soviet power and the dictatorship of the proletariat, is the *fundamental* task of the Communist Parties in all countries.

Second, the semi-proletarian or parcelized peasants, *i.e.,* those who obtain their livelihood, partly as wage laborers in agricultural and industrial capitalist enterprises, and partly by toiling on their own, or rented, plots of land, which are barely sufficient to provide them with some part of the means of subsistence for their families. This group of rural toilers is very numerous in all capitalist countries; its existence and special position are obscured by the representatives of the bourgeoisie and the yellow "Socialists" who belong to the Second International, some deliberately deceiving the workers, and some blindly submitting to routine, petty-bourgeois views, and confusing this group with the general mass of the "peasantry" as a whole. This bourgeois deception of the workers is most observed in Germany and in France; but is also observed in America and other countries. If the work of the Communist Party is properly organized, this group will become its assured adherent, for the conditions of the semi-proletarians are very hard and they stand to gain enormously and immediately from the Soviet power and the dictatorship of the proletariat.

Third, the small peasantry, *i.e.,* the small tillers of the soil who possess, either as their own property, or rent, small plots of land which enable them to meet the requirements of their families and their farms without hiring outside labor. This stratum, as such, undoubtedly stands to gain from the victory of the proletariat which will immediately and fully give it: (a) relief from the payment of rent or share of the crop (for example, the métayers in France, Italy and other countries) to the big landlords; (b) relief from mortgages; (c) relief from the numerous forms of oppression by and dependence upon the big landlords (use of forest lands, etc.); (d) immediate assistance for their farms from the proletarian state (facilities for using agricultural implements and some of the buildings on the big capitalist farms expropriated by the proletariat, the immediate transformation by the proletarian state of the village cooperatives and agricultural cooperative societies from organizations which, under capitalism, mostly serve the rich and middle peasants, into organizations that will primarily assist the poor, *i.e.,* the proletarians, the semi-proletarians, small peasants, etc.), and many other forms of assistance.

At the same time the Communist Party must clearly realize that in the period of transition from capitalism to Communism *i.e.,* in the period of the dictatorship of the proletariat, this stratum, or at all events, part of it, will inevitably incline towards unlimited freedom to trade and freedom to enjoy the rights of private property, for, being already (although in a small degree) sellers of consumers' goods, this stratum has been corrupted by profiteering and proprietary habits. However, if a firm proletarian policy is pursued, and if the victorious proletariat thoroughly and resolutely settles accounts with the big landlords and the big peasants, the vacillation of this stratum cannot be considerable and cannot alter the fact that, on the whole, it will be on the side of the proletarian revolution.

Taken together, the three groups of the rural population enumerated above constitute the majority of this population in all capitalist countries. Therefore, the success of the proletarian revolution is fully assured, not only in the towns, but also in the rural districts. There is a widespread opposite view; but this view only persists, firstly, because of the deception systematically practiced by bourgeois science and statistics, which do everything to obscure the wide gulf that separates the above-mentioned classes in the rural districts from the exploiters, the landlords and capitalists, and which also separates the semi-proletarians and small peasants from the big peasants; and secondly, it persists because of the inability and lack of desire of the heroes of the yellow, Second International, and the "labor aristocracy" in the advanced countries, which has been corrupted by imperialist privileges, to conduct genuine, proletarian work of revolutionary propaganda, agitation and organization among the rural poor; all the attention of the opportunists has been concentrated on inventing theoretical and practical compromises with the bourgeoisie, including the big and middle peasants (concerning whom see below) and not on the revolutionary overthrow of the bourgeois government and the bourgeoisie by the proletariat; thirdly, this view persists because of the persistent failure to understand – so persistent as to be equivalent to a prejudice (connected with all other bourgeois-democratic and parliamentary prejudices) – the truth which has been fully proved in theory by Marxism and fully confirmed by the experience of the proletarian revolution in Russia, *viz.,* that although all the three above-enumerated categories of the rural population – which are incredibly downtrodden, disunited, crushed and doomed to exist in semi-barbarous conditions in all, even the most advanced countries – are economically, socially, and culturally interested in the victory of socialism, they are capable of resolutely supporting the revolutionary proletariat only *after* the latter has won political power, only *after* it has resolutely settled accounts with the big landlords and capitalists, only *after* these downtrodden people see *in practice* that they have an organized leader and defender sufficiently strong and firm to assist and lead them, to show them the sure path.

V. I. Lenin, *Selected Works,* Russian edition, Vol. X.

Only the town and industrial proletariat, led by the Communist Party, can rescue the toiling masses of the village from the bondage of capital and of large-scale landlord ownership of land, from ruin and from the imperialist wars which will inevitably recur again and again as long as the capitalist regime endures. There is no salvation for the toiling masses of the village except in an alliance with the Communist proletariat, in unreserved support of its revolutionary struggle to throw off the yoke of the landlord (large landholders) and of the bourgeoisie.

On the other hand, the industrial workers will be unable to fulfill their world-historic mission of liberating mankind from the yoke of capital and from wars, if they confine themselves within the narrow circle of their guild and craft interests and, in a self-satisfied manner, restrict their efforts to improving their at times tolerable, petty-bourgeois conditions.

That is just what happens in many advanced countries with the "labor aristocracy," which forms the basis for the would-be Socialist parties of the Second International, in reality, however, constituting the worst enemies of Socialism, traitors to Socialism, petty-bourgeois chauvinists, agents of the bourgeoisie within the working-class movement. The proletariat becomes a truly revolutionary class, truly socialist in its actions, only when it comes out as and assumes the role of vanguard of all the toilers and exploited, of their leader in the struggle for the overthrow of the exploiters. But this is unfeasible without carrying the class struggle into the village, without uniting the toiling masses of the village around the Communist Party of the town proletariat, without the education of the former by the latter.

V. I. Lenin, "Preliminary Draft of the Theses on the Agrarian Question," *Collected Works*, Russian edition, Vol. XXV.

D. Role of the National Liberation Movements in the Proletarian Revolution – The National Liberation Movement as the Reserve and Component Part of the World Socialist Revolution

It becomes entirely clear that the socialist revolution which is drawing near for the whole world will in no wise consist only in the victory of the proletariat in each country over its own bourgeoisie. This would be possible if the revolution occurred easily and quickly. We know that the imperialists will not permit this, that all countries are armed against their domestic Bolshevism and think only of how they might conquer Bolshevism at home. Therefore civil war, to which the old socialist-compromisers are drawn, on the side of the bourgeoisie, is being born in each country. In this way the socialist revolution will not be only and mainly a struggle of the revolutionary proletarians in each country against their own bourgeoisie – no, it will be a struggle of all colonies and countries oppressed by imperialism, of all dependent countries, against international imperialism. In the program of our Party, which was adopted in March of last year, we, in characterizing the approach of the world-wide social revolution, said that the civil war of the toilers against the imperialists and exploiters in all advanced countries begins to unite with the national war against the international imperialists. This is being confirmed by the course of the revolution and will be confirmed more and more. In the East it will be the same.... The peoples of the East are waking up to the fact that they must act practically and that each people must decide the fate of all humanity.

This is why I think that in the history of the development of the world revolution, which, judging by the beginning, will continue for many years and will demand much labor, it will be your lot to play a great role in the revolutionary struggle, in the revolutionary movement, and to merge this struggle in our struggle against international imperialism. Your participation in the international revolution places you before a complicated and difficult task, the solution of which will serve as the basis for the common success, because here for the first time the majority of the population comes to independent action and will be an active factor in the struggle for the overthrow of international imperialism.

Most nations of the East are in a worse position than Russia, the most backward country in Europe, but in the struggle against the remnants of feudalism and capitalism we have succeeded in uniting the Russian peasants and workers, and our struggle passed so easily because the peasants and the workers united against capital and feudalism, and here the tie with the peoples of the East is particularly important because the majority of the peoples of the East are typical representatives of the laboring mass – not workers who have gone through the school of imperialist factories and mills, but typical representatives of the toiling, exploited mass of peasants who suffer from medieval oppression. The Russian Revolution has shown how the proletarians who have been victorious over capitalism, who have been welded with the many millions of scattered toiling peasants, victoriously rose against medieval oppression. And now it will be the lot of the Soviet Republic to group around itself all the awakened peoples of the East in order to wage a struggle jointly with them against international imperialism. Here you are confronted with the task which before did not confront the Communists of the whole world: Relying on general Communist theory and practice and conforming to the peculiar conditions which do not exist in European countries, you need the ability to apply this theory and practice to conditions when the peasantry constitutes the bulk, when it is necessary to decide the task of struggling not against capitalism but against medieval remnants. This is a difficult and peculiar task, but it is particularly remunerative because the mass which is drawn into the struggle has not yet participated in the struggle and on the other hand, thanks to the organization of the communist nuclei in the East you are enabled to establish the closest contact with the Third International. You must find the peculiar forms of this alliance between the foremost proletarians of the whole world and the toiling and exploited masses of the East which partly live under medieval conditions. We have carried out in our country on a small scale what you will realize in big countries on a large scale.

V. I. Lenin, "Report at the Second All-Russian Congress of Communist Organizations of the Peoples of the East," *Collected Works,* Russian edition, Vol. XXIV.

E. The United Front as the Tactic for the Winning Over
of the Workers for Revolution

To the Workers of All Countries!

The crisis continues to develop and deepen. Unemployment is increasing without interruption, hunger and misery are seizing ever fresh strata of the workers. The capitalist offensive is assuming ever sharper forms. The bourgeoisie are preparing to launch a campaign against all the political and economic achievements of the working class.

Fascist reaction is seizing one country after another. The establishment of the open fascist dictatorship in Germany has inexorably confronted millions of workers of all countries with the question of the necessity of organizing the united front of struggle against the fascist offensive of the bourgeoisie, and above all against that of the German bourgeoisie, who, step by step, are robbing the working class of all their economic and political achievements and attempting to crush the workers' movement with the most brutal methods of terror.

The main obstacle to the formation of the united front of struggle of the Communist and Social-Democratic workers was and is the policy of collaboration with the bourgeoisie conducted by the Social-Democratic Parties, who have now exposed the international proletariat to the blows of the class enemy. This policy of class collaboration with the bourgeoisie, known as the so-called policy of the "lesser evil," has led in practice to the triumph of fascist reaction in Germany.

The Communist International and the Communist Parties of all countries have repeatedly declared their readiness to join in a common fight along with the Social-Democratic workers against the capitalist offensive, against political reaction and war danger. The Communist Parties were the organizers of the common fight of the

Communist, Social-Democratic and non-Party workers in spite of the leaders of the Social-Democratic Parties, who systematically disrupted the united front of the working masses. On July 20, last year, the Communist Party of Germany, after the Prussian Social-Democratic government had been driven out by Papen, proposed to the Social-Democratic Party of Germany and the A.D.G.B. (German General Federation of Trade Unions) to organize a common strike against fascism. But the Social-Democratic Party and the Trade Unions (A.D.G.B.), with the approval of the whole of the Second International, described the proposal to organize a common strike as a provocation. The Communist Party of Germany repeated its proposal of common action at the moment when Hitler seized power; it called upon the Central Committee of the Social-Democratic Party and the Executive Committee of the A.D.G.B. jointly to organize the resistance to fascism, but this time also met with a refusal. Nay, more, when in November, last year, the Berlin transport workers unanimously went on strike against a wage reduction, the Social-Democratic Party sabotaged the united front struggle. The whole practice of the international labor movement is full of similar examples.

On February 19 last the bureau of the Labor and Social International published a declaration on the readiness of the Social-Democratic Parties affiliated to this International to form a united front with the Communists in order to fight against the fascist reaction in Germany. This declaration stands in sharp contradiction to the whole of the previous actions of the L.S.I. and Social-Democratic Parties. The whole policy and activity of the L.S.I. hitherto justifies the Communist International and the Communist Parties in putting *no* faith in the sincerity of the declaration of the L.S.I. Bureau, which makes its proposal at a moment when in a number of countries, and before all in Germany, the working masses are taking into their own hands the organizing of the united front. In spite of this, however, the Executive Committee of the Communist International, in view of the attacks upon the working class of Germany by fascism, which is unchaining all the forces of world reaction, calls upon all Communist Parties to make yet another attempt to set up the united front of struggle with the Socialist-Democratic workers through the medium of the Social-Democratic Parties. The E.C.C.I. makes this attempt in the firm conviction that the united front of the working class against the bourgeoisie will be able to repel the offensive of capital and fascism and extraordinarily to accelerate the inevitable end of all capitalist exploitation.

Owing to the peculiarity of the conditions, as well as the differences in the concrete fighting tasks confronting the working class in the various countries, an agreement between the Communist and Social-Democratic Parties for definite actions against the bourgeoisie can be carried out most successfully within the confines of each individual country. The E.C.C.I. therefore recommends the Communist Parties of the various countries to approach the central committees of the Social-Democratic Parties belonging to the L.S.I. with proposals regarding joint actions against fascism and against the offensive of capital. These negotiations must be based on the most elementary prerequisites for the common fight against the offensive of capital and fascism. Without a concrete program of action against the bourgeoisie any agreement between the parties would be directed against the interests of the working class. The Executive Committee of the Communist International therefore proposes the following points as a basis for an agreement of joint action:

(a) The Communist and Social-Democrats commence at once to organize and carry out defensive action against the attacks of fascism and reaction on the political, trade union, cooperative and other workers' organizations, on the workers' press, on the freedom of meetings, demonstrations and strikes. They shall organize common defense against the armed attacks of the fascist bands by carrying out mass protests, street demonstrations and political mass strikes; they shall proceed to organize committees of action in the workshops and factories, the Labor Exchanges and the workers' quarters, as well as to organize self-defense groups.

(b) Communists and Social-Democrats shall commence at once to organize the protest of the workers, with the aid of meetings, demonstrations and strikes, against any wage reductions, against worsening of the working conditions, against attacks on social insurance, against the cutting down of unemployment benefit, against dismissals from the factories.

(c) In the adoption and practical carrying out of these two conditions the E.C.C.I. considers it possible to recommend the Communist Parties, during the time of common fight against capital and fascism, to refrain from making attacks on Social-Democratic organizations. The most ruthless fight must be conducted against all those who violate the conditions of the agreement in carrying out the united front, as against strikebreakers who disrupt the united front of the workers.

These conditions, which are put forward for acceptance by the parties of the L.S.I., apply also to those parties which, like the I.L.P., for example, have proposed to the Comintern the organization of the united front of struggle.

The Executive Committee of the Communist International, which makes these proposals before the international working class, calls upon all Communist Parties, and in the first place on the Communist Party of Germany, immediately and without waiting for the results of negotiations and agreements with the Social-Democracy with regard to a common fight, to proceed to organize joint fighting committees with Social-Democratic workers and with workers of all other tendencies.

The Communists have proved through their long years of struggle that they stand, and will stand, not in words but in deeds, in the front ranks of the fight for the united front in class actions against the bourgeoisie.

The Executive Committee of the Communist International firmly believes that the Social-Democratic and non-Party workers, regardless of what attitude the Social-Democratic leaders adopt to the setting up of the united front, will overcome all obstacles and, together with the Communists, set up the united front not in words but in deeds.

Precisely at the present moment, when German fascism has organized a monstrous provocation (setting fire to the Reichstag, forging documents about an alleged Communist insurrection, etc.) in order to crush the workers' movement in Germany, every worker must recognize his class duty in the fight against the capitalist offensive and fascist reaction.

Down with fascist reaction and terror against the working class! For the united front of struggle of the proletariat!

Proletarians of all countries, unite for the fight against the capitalist offensive and fascism!

Appeal of the Executive Committee of the Communist International, March 5, 1933.

4. Exposure of the Social-Democratic Phraseology as to the Prerequisites of Socialism and "Capitalism Growing Peacefully Into Socialism"*

A. Exposure of the Kautskian Theory of Ultra-Imperialism

The notorious theory of "ultra-imperialism," invented by Kautsky, is equally reactionary in character....

Indeed, it is enough to keep clearly in mind well known and indisputable facts to become convinced of the complete falsity of the perspectives which Kautsky is trying to hold out to the German workers (and the workers of all countries). Let us take India, Indo-China and China. It is well known that these three colonial and semi-colonial countries, inhabited by six or seven hundred million human beings, are subjected to the exploitation of the finance capital of several imperialist powers: Great Britain, France, Japan, the United States. Let us assume that these imperialist countries form alliances against one another in order to protect and extend their possessions, interests, and "spheres of influence" in these Asiatic states; these will be "inter-imperialist," or "ultra-imperialist" alliances. Let us assume that *all* the imperialist powers conclude an alliance for the "peaceful" partition of these Asiatic countries; this alliance would be "internationally united finance capital." Actual examples of such an alliance may be seen in the history of the twentieth century, for instance, in the relations of the powers with China. We ask, is it "conceivable," assuming that the capitalist system is preserved (and this is precisely the assumption that Kautsky does make), that such alliances would not be short-lived, that they would preclude friction, conflicts and struggle in any and every possible form?

It suffices to state this question clearly to make any other reply than a negative one impossible; for there can be *no other* conceivable basis, under capitalism, for partition of spheres of influence, of interests, of colonies, etc., than a calculation of the *strength* of the participants, their general economic, financial, military and other strength. Now, the relative strength of these participants is not

---

* On the role of Social-Democracy at the present stage, see the subtitle of Georgi Dimitroff's speech at the Seventh World Congress of the Communist International: *The Role of Social-Democracy and Its Attitude Toward the United Front of the Proletariat. – Ed.*

changing uniformly, for under capitalism there cannot be an even development of different undertakings, trusts, branches of industry or countries. Half a century ago, Germany was a pitiable nonentity as compared with Britain of that time so far as capitalist strength was concerned. The same with Japan as compared with Russia. Is it "conceivable" that in ten or twenty years' time the relative strength of the imperialist powers will have remained unchanged? Absolutely inconceivable.

Therefore, "inter-imperialist" or "ultra-imperialist" alliances, no matter in what form these alliances be concluded, whether of one imperialist coalition against another or of a general alliance of *all* the imperialist powers, *inevitably* can be only "breathing spells" between wars. Peaceful alliances prepare the ground for wars and in their turn grow out of war. One is the condition of the other, giving rise to alternating forms of peaceful and non-peaceful struggle *on one and the same* basis, that of imperialist connections and inter-relations of world economics and world politics.

...An American writer, Hill, in his *History of Diplomacy in the International Development of Europe,* points out in his preface the following periods of modern diplomatic history: (1) the revolutionary period; (2) the constitutional movement; (3) the present period of "commercial imperialism."[*]

Another writer divides the history of Great Britain's "foreign policy" since 1870 into four periods: (1) the Asiatic period: struggle against Russia's advance in Central Asia towards India; (2) the African period (approximately 1885-1902): struggles against France over the partition of Africa (the Fashoda affair, 1898, a hair's-breadth from a war with France); (3) the second Asiatic period (treaty with Japan against Russia); and (4) the "European" period, chiefly directed against Germany.

"The political skirmishes of outposts are fought on the financial field," wrote Riesser, the banker, in 1905, showing how French finance capital operating in Italy was preparing the way for a political alliance between the two countries, how a struggle was developing between Germany and Britain over Persia, a struggle among all the European capitalists over Chinese loans, etc. Behold, the living reality of peaceful "ultra-imperialist" alliances in their indissoluble

---

[*] David Jayne Hill, *A History of Diplomacy in the International Development of Europe*, Vol. I, p. x.

connection with ordinary imperialist conflicts!

The glossing over of the deepest contradictions of imperialism by Kautsky, which inevitably becomes a decking-out of imperialism, leaves its traces also in this writer's critique of the political features of imperialism. Imperialism is the epoch of finance capital and of monopolies which introduce everywhere the striving for domination, not for freedom. The result of these tendencies is reaction all along the line, whatever the political system, and extreme intensification of antagonisms in this domain also. Particularly acute also becomes national oppression and the striving for annexation, *i.e.*, the violation of national independence (for annexation is nothing else than a violation of the right of nations to self-determination). Hilferding justly draws attention to the relation between imperialism and the intensification of national oppression.

> But in the newly opened-up countries – he writes – the imported capital intensifies antagonisms and excites the constantly growing resistance of the peoples who are awakened to national consciousness against the intruders. This resistance can easily become transformed into dangerous measures directed against foreign capital. Former social relations become completely revolutionized. The agrarian thousand-year-old insularity of the "nations beyond the pale of history" is being shattered, and they themselves are drawn into the capitalist whirlpool. Capitalism itself gradually provides the vanquished with the ways and means for their emancipation. And they set out to achieve that goal which once was the highest for the European nations: the construction of a national united state as a means to economic and cultural freedom. This movement for independence threatens European capital precisely in its most valuable and most promising fields of exploitation, and European capital can maintain its domination only by constantly increasing its military forces. [*]

To this must be added that it is not only in newly opened-up countries, but also in the old ones, that imperialism is leading to annexation, to increased national oppression, and, consequently, also to

***

[*] Rudolf Hilferding, *Das Finanzkapital* (Finance Capital), 2nd ed., pp. 433-434.

more stubborn resistance. While objecting to the growth of political reaction caused by imperialism, Kautsky leaves in the dark a question which has become very urgent, that of the impossibility of unity with the opportunists in the epoch of imperialism. While objecting to annexations, he presents his objections in such a form as will be most acceptable and least offensive to the opportunists. He addresses himself directly to a German audience, yet he obscures the most timely and important points, for instance, that Alsace-Lorraine is an annexation by Germany. In order to appraise this "mental aberration" of Kautsky's, we shall take the following example. Let us suppose that a Japanese is condemning the annexation of the Philippine Islands by the Americans. Are there many who will believe that he is protesting because he abhors annexations in general, and not because he himself has a desire to annex the Philippines? And shall we not be constrained to admit that the "fight" the Japanese is waging against annexations can be regarded as sincere and politically honest only if he fights against the annexation of Korea by Japan, and demands for Korea freedom of separation from Japan?

Kautsky's theoretical analysis of imperialism and his economic and political critique of imperialism are permeated *through and through* with a spirit absolutely irreconcilable with Marxism, a spirit that obscures and glosses over the most basic contradictions of imperialism, and strives to preserve at all costs the crumbling unity with opportunism in the European labor movement.

V. I. Lenin, *Imperialism, the Highest Stage of Capitalism*, Little Lenin Library, Vol. 15, pp. 107-110.

B. The Struggle Against the Menshevik Theory of the Preconditions of the Proletarian Revolution and the Appraisal of the October Revolution

These days I ran through Sukhanov's notes on the Revolution. What strikes one most is the pedantry of all our petty-bourgeois democrats as well as of all the heroes of the Second International. One is struck by their slavish imitativeness of the past, not to mention that they are unusually cowardly, that even the best of them subsist on little reservations when it is a question of the slightest deviation from the German model, not to mention this quality of all petty-bourgeois democrats, sufficiently manifested by them throughout the Revolution.

They all call themselves Marxists, but their understanding of Marxism is pedantic to an impossible degree. They have absolutely failed to understand what is decisive in Marxism, *viz.,* its revolutionary dialectics. Even Marx's direct instructions that in moments of revolution maximum flexibility is required are absolutely unintelligible to them, and they have even failed to note, for instance, Marx's instruction in his correspondence referring, it may be remembered, to 1856, when he expressed the hope of uniting a peasant war in Germany, able to create a revolutionary situation, with the labor movement – even this direct instruction they evade, walk round and round it, up and down like a cat circling around a bowl of hot milk.

In their entire conduct they reveal themselves as cowardly reformists who are afraid to withdraw from the bourgeoisie and so much the more to break with it, while at the same time they cover up their cowardice with the most reckless phrase-mongering and boasting. But even purely theoretically one is struck by the complete inability of all of them to understand the following consideration of Marxism: they have seen hitherto a definite path of development of capitalism and bourgeois democracy in western Europe. And they cannot imagine that this road can be considered a model *mutatis mutandis*[*] but only with a few changes (absolutely unimportant ones from the point of view of world history).

First: the revolution, connected with the first world imperialist war. In such a revolution, new features, or features modified precisely in dependence upon the war, were bound to manifest themselves, because there never yet had been any such war anywhere in the world under such circumstances. So far we have seen that the bourgeoisie of the richest countries is unable to establish "normal" bourgeois relations after this war, but our reformists, petty bourgeois who put on the mien of revolutionaries, consider normal bourgeois relations to be the limit (which you may not overstep) and this "norm" they understand in an extremely stereotyped and narrow sense.

Second: All thought of the fact that under the general law of development of universal history, individual stages of development, representing peculiarities either in the form or the method of this development, are not at all excluded but on the contrary presup-

---

[*] Making the necessary changes. – *Ed.*

posed, is absolutely alien to them. For instance, it does not even occur to them that Russia, which lies on the borderline between civilized countries and countries that have been finally drawn into civilization for the first time by this war, the countries of the entire East, the countries outside of Europe – that Russia therefore might and was bound to show some peculiarities, conforming, of course, to the general line of world development, but distinguishing its revolution from all preceding ones of the West-European countries, and introducing some partial innovations when passing on to the eastern countries.

For instance, they have an infinitely trite argument which they learnt by heart at the time West-European Social-Democracy was developing, and which claims that we have not grown up to socialism, that we do not have the objective economic prerequisites for socialism, as various "learned" gentlemen among them express themselves. And it does not occur to any one to ask himself: Could not a people, on encountering a revolutionary situation, such as took shape in the first imperialist war – could it not, under the influence of hopelessness of its position, take up such a struggle as would open up to it at least some chances of winning for itself not quite usual conditions for the further development of civilization.

"Russia has not attained the high level of development of its productive forces under which socialism is possible." All the heroes of the Second International, including, of course, Sukhanov, fuss over this sentence exactly like a child over a new toy. This undisputed sentence they rehash in a thousand different forms and they think it is decisive for an appraisal of our revolution.

Well, and what if the peculiarity of the situation put Russia, in the first place into the world imperialist war, in which all somewhat influential West-European countries are involved, placed its development on the brink of the revolutions of the East which are beginning and in part have already begun, under such conditions that we could realize precisely that union between the "peasant war" and the labor movement, which a "Marxist" like Marx, writing in 1856 regarding Prussia, considered as one of the possible perspectives.

What if the complete lack of a way out of the situation, which thereby increases the forces of the workers and the peasants tenfold, opened up to us the possibility of a transition to the creation of the basic premises of civilization different from those in all the remaining West-European states? Would the general line of development of world history be changed on that account? Would the principal correlations of the principle classes be changed on that account in each state which is being drawn and has been drawn into the general march of world history?

If a definite level of culture is required to create socialism (although no one can say what that definite "level of culture" is), why cannot we begin from the beginning with the conquest, in a revolutionary manner, of the prerequisites for this definite level, and *afterwards,* on the basis of the workers' and peasants' power, and of the Soviet order, move to overtake other nations?

V. I. Lenin, "Concerning Our Revolution," *Collected Works,* Vol. XXVII, Russian edition, pp. 398-400.

C. Struggle Against the Social-Democratic Theory of the Peaceful Growing of Capitalism Into Socialism

But to what depths of stupidity, baseness and vileness the Austrian Social-Democrats have sunk is demonstrated very clearly by the whole policy of Renner and similar Austrian Seheidemanns, who are aided – in part through extreme stupidity and lack of character – by the Otto Bauers and Friedrich Adlers, the latter having become plain traitors.*

---

* Editor's Note: The numerous utterances of contemporary Social-Democratic theoreticians, despite their diversity, are united by a common bourgeois-reformist policy of class peace at any price, of the consolidation of capitalism.

Here is for instance what Kautsky writes on calling the workers "to socialism" by means of consolidating capitalism from every aspect:

"In times of prosperity wages as well as profits grow. The proletariat must aim to have production in the capitalist enterprises proceed in future as smoothly as heretofore....

"The greatest and in the long run the sole effective economic driving force is *interest,* whether personal or collective, and not *compulsion.*

"If a proletarian regime wants successfully to counteract the attempts at sabotage of those capitalists whom it still needs, it must imbue them with an interest in the uninterrupted operation and constant improvement of their enterprises. This is impossible if every enterprise that is being socialized is *confiscated.* This can only be attained if a *fair compensation is paid* as soon as steps are taken to socialize it. That is, this compensation should be a remuneration for those who will have kept their enterprises up to date and will have managed them with good commercial success.... The more economic concussions are avoided in doing so, the more one achieves through an amicable understanding, the less one must resort to compulsory expropriation, even if with compensation, the better." (Karl Kautsky, *The Proletarian Revolution and Its Program,* Stuttgart, 1922, pp. 183, 186.)

And further on:

"The more the capitalist method of production prospers and flourishes, the better the prospects of the socialist regime which will take the place of the capitalist regime."

The notorious industrial democracy plan is likewise built on the idea of collaboration with the capitalists at any price at all.

The following is the way in which the prospects of industrial democracy are pictured by Paul Hörnberg, one of the social-democratic theoreticians, who endeavors to combine the industrial democracy plan with the Hilferdingian policy of organizing state capitalism:

"The expansion of economic activity of the state institutions, the increase in the authority granted to the state economic council,, the institution of district economic councils and economic chambers, the transfer of entire industrial branches of the control of the state, or, speaking more briefly, all measures which strengthen the beginnings of real leadership of economy, will be the most important and most signal preparation of industrial democracy."

It is quite obvious that Bauer's clever "original functional democracy" is built on the same principles.

By "functional democracy" Bauer means "the demand that the government be controlled by citizens united and classified according to their trades, places of work and social and political-economic functions."

The program of the Communist International characterizes the ideology of modern Social-Democracy as follows:

"In the sphere of theory, social-democracy has utterly and completely betrayed Marxism, having traversed the road from revisionism to complete liberal bourgeois reformism and avowed social-imperialism: it has substituted in place of the Marxian theory of the contradictions of capitalism the bourgeois theory of its harmonious development; it has pigeon-holed the theory of crisis and of the pauperization of the proletariat; it has turned the flaming and menacing theory of class struggle into prosaic advocacy of class peace; it has exchanged the theory of growing class antagonisms for the petty-bourgeois fairy-

Take as an example Otto Bauer's pamphlet, *Der Weg zum Sozialismus* (*Path to Socialism*). I have before me the Berlin edition published by the *Freiheit,* evidently the organ of the Independent Party, which stands on the same low, trivial, and abject level as the

---

tale about the 'democratization' of capital; in place of the theory of the inevitability of war under capitalism it has substituted the bourgeois deceit of pacifism and the lying propaganda of 'ultra-imperialism'; it has exchanged the theory of the revolutionary downfall of capitalism for the counterfeit coinage of 'sound' capitalism transforming itself peacefully into socialism; it has replaced revolution by evolution, the destruction of the bourgeois state by its active upbuilding, the theory of proletarian dictatorship by the theory of coalition with the bourgeoisie, the doctrine of international proletarian solidarity – by preaching defense of the imperialist fatherland; for Marxian dialectical materialism it has substituted the idealist philosophy and is now engaged in picking up the crumbs of religion that fall from the table of the bourgeoisie."
(*Program of the Communist International,* Part VI, Section I.)

In the same section of the Program an appraisal of Bauer's "Left" Social-Democracy is also given:

"Austro-Marxism is a special form of Social-Democratic reformism. Being a component part of the 'Left' Wing of Social-Democracy, Austro-Marxism represents the most subtle form of deceiving the toiling masses. By prostituting Marxian terminology and at the same time decisively breaking with the principles of revolutionary Marxism (Kautskianism, Machism, etc., of the 'Austro-Marxists' in the field of philosophy), flirting with religion, copying from the British reformists the theory of 'functional democracy,' advocating the point of view of 'the building of a republic,' *i.e.,* the building of a bourgeois state, Austro-Marxism recommends 'the cooperation of classes' in the period of so-called 'equilibrium of class forces,' *i.e.,* just when the revolutionary crisis matures. This theory denotes an approval of coalition with the bourgeoisie for the overthrow of the proletarian revolution under the guise of defending 'democracy' against the attack of reaction. Objectively and in practice, the force conceded by the Austro-Marxists, in case of an attack by reaction, is transformed into the force of reaction against the revolution of the proletariat. The 'functional role' of Austro-Marxism consists in deceiving the workers already going to Communism, and therefore Austro-Marxism is a dangerous enemy of the proletariat, more dangerous than the open adherents of predatory social imperialism."

51

pamphlet.

It suffices to glance at a few places in Section 9 ("Expropriation of the Expropriators"):

"....Expropriation... cannot and should not be carried out in the form of a harsh, brutal confiscation of the property of the capitalists and landlords; for in this form it could not be carried out except at the price of a wholesale destruction of the means of production, which would pauperize the masses themselves and choke the sources of national income. Expropriation of the expropriators should rather be carried out in an orderly, regulated manner... by means of taxation."

And the learned gentleman gives an example of how by means of taxes "four-ninths" of their income could be taken from the possessing classes....

Is not that enough? As for me, after these words (and I began reading the pamphlet with Section 9) I read no more and, unless there is some special need, do not intend to read more of Mr. Otto Bauer's pamphlet. For it is clear that this best of social-traitors is at best, a learned fool, absolutely beyond hope.

This is an example of a pedant, through and through petty-bourgeois in spirit. He used to write useful learned books and articles prior to the war, admitting "theoretically" that the class struggle may become accentuated to the point of civil war. He even took part (if I am correctly informed) in the formulation of the Basle manifesto of 1912, which plainly foresaw a *proletarian revolution* in connection with precisely the war which broke out in 1914.

But when actually confronted by this proletarian revolution, then there came out uppermost his nature as a pedant and philistine, who took fright and *began to sprinkle the raging revolution with the oil of reformist phrases.*

He thoroughly learned by heart (pedants do not know how to think; they know how to memorize; they can learn by heart) that it is theoretically possible to expropriate the expropriators without confiscation. He kept on repeating this. He learned this by heart. He knew this by heart in 1912. He repeated it from memory in 1919.

He does not know how to think. After the imperialist war – and moreover after such a war which even brought the victors to the brink of ruin – after the beginning of civil war in a number of countries, after facts on an international scale have proven the inevitability of the transformation of the imperialist war into a civil war, to preach, in the year of our Lord 1919, in the city of Vienna, about the "orderly" and "regulated" taking away from the capitalists of "four-ninths" of their income – to do this one must either be mentally ailing or resemble that old hero of the classic German poem who passes with ecstasy "from book to book...."

This most kind-hearted soul – who probably is a most virtuous father of a family, a most honest citizen, a most conscientious reader and writer of learned books – has entirely forgotten one tiny trifle. He has forgotten that such an "orderly" and "regulated" transition to Socialism (a transition, undoubtedly, most advantageous for the "people," speaking abstractly) presupposes the absolute stability of the victory of the proletariat, the absolute hopelessness of the position of the capitalists, the absolute necessity for them to show and their readiness to show the most conscientious submission.

Is such a concurrence of circumstances possible?

Speaking theoretically, *i.e.,* in the present case entirely abstractly: yes, of course. For example, let us assume that in nine countries, including all the Great Powers, the Wilsons, the Lloyd Georges, the Millerands, and the other heroes of capitalism already find themselves in a similar position to that of our Yudenich, Kolchak, and Denikin with their ministers. Let us assume that in a tenth small country, subsequent to this, the capitalists propose to the workers: Come, we will help you conscientiously, subordinating ourselves to your decisions, to carry out an "orderly" and peaceful (without destruction!) "expropriation of the expropriators," receiving in return five-ninths of our former income the first year, four-ninths – the second year.

It is quite conceivable that, under the conditions I have indicated, the capitalists of the tenth country might make such a proposal in one of the smallest and most "peaceful" countries, and likewise it would not be reprehensible on the part of the workers of this country, if they should consider this proposal in a business-like way and (after some haggling, for a merchant can't get along without overcharging) should accept it.

Perhaps now after this popular explanation even the learned Otto Bauer and the philosopher (as successful a philosopher as statesman) Friedrich Adler may understand what it is all about.

Not yet? Is it not clear?

Consider for a moment, my dear Otto Bauer, my dear Friedrich Adler: Is the present situation of world capitalism and its leaders similar to the position of Yudenich, Kolchak, and Denikin in Russia?

No, it is not similar. In Russia the capitalists have been defeated after desperate resistance on their part. In all the rest of the world they are still in power. They are the masters.

If you, my dear Otto Bauer and Friedrich Adler, still do not understand what it is all about, I shall put it in a still more popular form.

Imagine that at the time when Yudenich was at the gates of Petrograd, when Kolchak had control of the Urals and Denikin the whole of the Ukraine, when the pockets of all three of these heroes were stuffed with cables from Wilson, Lloyd George, Millerand and Co. about the dispatching of money, cannons, officers, soldiers – imagine that at such a time there had come to Yudenich, Kolchak, or Denikin a representative of the Russian workers and said: We, the workers, are the majority. We shall give you five-ninths of your income, but later we shall take away this also in an "orderly" and peaceful manner. Come, let's close the deal, "without destruction." Agreed?

If this representative of the workers had been poorly dressed, and if a Russian general, such as Denikin, alone had received him, he would probably have been sent off to the madhouse or simply chased away.

V. I. Lenin, "Notes of a Publicist," *Collected Works,* Vol. XXV.

.

II. UNEVEN ECONOMIC AND POLITICAL DEVELOPMENT OF CAPITALISM, BREAK IN THE CHAIN OF IMPERIALISM AT THE WEAKEST LINK AND THE POSSIBILITY OF THE VICTORY OF SOCIALISM IN ONE COUNTRY

1. Stalin on the Leninist Teaching of the Uneven Development of Imperialism, the Weakest Link and the Possibility of the Victory of Socialism in One Country

In studying imperialism, especially in the period of the war, Lenin arrived at the law of the unevenness, of the spasmodic character of the economic and political development of the capitalist countries. According to this law, the development of enterprises, trusts, branches of industry and of separate countries proceeds, not evenly, not according to an established order of succession, not in such a way that one trust, one branch of industry or one country continually proceeds in advance of the others, while other trusts or countries lag behind one another, but spasmodically, with interruptions in the development of some countries and leaps ahead in the development of others. Under these conditions the "quite legitimate" ambition of the countries that are lagging behind to preserve their old positions and the equally "legitimate" ambition of the countries that are leaping forward to seize new positions leads to a situation in which armed clashes among the imperialist countries are an inevitable necessity. Such was the case, for example, with Germany, which, half a century ago, in comparison with France and England, represented a backward country. The same must be said of Japan, in comparison with Russia. It is a well-known fact, however, that by the beginning of the twentieth century Germany and Japan had leaped so far ahead that the first had succeeded in overtaking France and had begun to press England hard on the world market, while Japan was overtaking Russia. From these contradictions arose, as is well-known, the recent imperialist war.

This law proceeds from the following:

1. "Capitalism has grown into a world system of colonial oppression and of the financial strangulation of the overwhelming majority of the people of the world by a handful of the 'advanced' countries." (Lenin, Preface to French edition of *Imperialism.*)

2. "And this 'booty' is shared between two or three powerful

world pirates armed to the teeth (America, Great Britain, Japan) who involve the whole world in *their* war over the sharing of *their* booty." (*Ibid.*)

3. *The* growth of contradictions within the world system of financial oppression and the inevitability of armed clashes make the world front of imperialism vulnerable to revolution and make the piercing of this front by certain countries probable.

4. This breach is more likely to occur at such points, and in such countries, in which the chain of the imperialist front is weakest, that is to say, in which imperialism is least equipped and where it is easier for revolution to develop.

5. In view of this, the victory of socialism in one country, even if this country is capitalistically less developed – while capitalism is preserved in other countries: – even if these countries are more highly developed capitalistically, is quite possible and probable.

Such are in brief the foundations of Lenin's theory of the proletarian revolution.

Joseph Stalin, "The Tactics of the Russian Communists," *The October Revolution.*

2. The Law of the Uneven Development of Capitalism and the Struggle Against the Trotskyist Negation of This Law

Wherein lies the difference between the old, pre-monopolistic capitalism and the new, monopolistic capitalism, if one is to express this difference in a few words?

It consists in the fact that development through free competition has given place to development through grandiose monopolistic unions of capitalists; that old, "cultural," "progressive" capitalism has given place to finance capital, to "decaying" capitalism; that the "peaceful" expansion of capitalism and its extension to "free" territories has given place to spasmodic development, to a development through the redivision of a world already divided, through the medium of military clashes between capitalist groups; that old capitalism, which as a whole had developed in an ascending line, has thus given place to moribund capitalism, to capitalism developing as a whole in a descending line.

Here is what Lenin says on this score:

"Let us recall what caused the change from the former 'peaceful' epoch of capitalism to the present imperialist epoch: free competition was replaced by monopolist capitalist combines, the world was divided up. It is obvious that both these facts (and factors) are really of world-wide significance: free trade and peaceful competition were possible and necessary as long as capital was in a position to enlarge its colonies without hindrance, and to seize unoccupied land in Africa, etc., as long as the concentration of capital was still slight and no monopolist undertakings, *i.e.,* undertakings of such magnitude as to dominate a whole branch of industry, existed. The appearance and growth of such monopolist undertakings make the free competition of former times impossible, cut the ground from under its feet, while the division of the world *compels* the capitalists to pass from peaceful expansion to armed struggle for the *redivision* of colonies and spheres of influence." (Lenin, *The Collapse of the Second International.*)

And further:

It is *impossible* to live in the old way, in the comparatively calm, cultured, peaceful surroundings of a capitalism that is *smoothly evolving* [My emphasis. – *J. S.*] and gradually spreading to new countries, for a new epoch has been ushered in. Finance Capital is *squeezing out*, and will squeeze out, the given country from the ranks of Great Powers, will deprive it of its colonies and spheres of influence. (Lenin, *ibid.*)

Hence Lenin's principal conclusion concerning the character of imperialist capitalism:

"It is clear why imperialism is *moribund* capitalism, the *transition* to socialism: monopoly, growing *out* of capitalism, is already the dying out of capitalism, the beginning of its transition to socialism. The tremendous *socialization* of labor by imperialism (what the apologetic bourgeois economists call 'interlocking') signifies the same thing." (Lenin, "Imperialism and the Split in the Socialist Movement," *Collected Works,* Vol. XIX.)

It is the misfortune of our opposition that it does not understand the full importance of this difference between pre-imperialist capitalism and imperialist capitalism.

Thus, the point of departure of the position of our Party is the recognition of the fact that present-day capitalism, imperialist capitalism, is moribund capitalism.

This, unfortunately, does not yet denote that capitalism is already dead. But it undoubtedly does denote that capitalism as a whole does not march to a revival but to its expiration, that capitalism as a whole is developing not in an ascending line but in a descending line.

From this general question issues the question of the uneven development in the period of imperialism.

What do Leninists usually speak of when they speak of the uneven development in the period of imperialism?

Do they not speak of the fact that a great difference exists in the level of development of the capitalist countries, that some countries lag behind others in their development, that this difference becomes greater and greater?

No, they do not. To confuse the uneven development under imperialism with the difference in the level of development of the capitalist countries means to fall into philistinism. This is precisely the philistinism into which the opposition fell, when at the Fifteenth Conference of the All-Russian Communist Party the question of the uneven *development* was confused with the question of the difference in the level of the economic position of the various capitalist countries. Proceeding precisely from this confusion, the opposition arrived at that time at the absolutely incorrect conclusion that the unevenness of the development was greater before than under imperialism. This is precisely the reason why at the Fifteenth Conference Comrade Trotsky said that in the nineteenth century this unevenness was *greater* than in the twentieth. (See the speech of Com. Trotsky at the Fifteenth Conference of the All-Russian C.P.) Comrade Zinoviev said the same thing at that time, asserting that "...it was not true that the unevenness of capitalist *development* before the beginning of the imperialist epoch was less." (See speech of Com. Zinoviev at the Fifteenth Conference of the All-Russian C.P.) It is true that now, after the discussion at the Fifteenth Conference, the opposition has found it necessary to change front, declaring in its speeches at the Enlarged Plenum of the E.C.C.I. something absolutely the opposite, or trying simply to keep silent about this mistake of theirs. Here is, for instance, the statement of Com. Trotsky in his speech at the Enlarged Plenum: "As far as the tempo of development is concerned, imperialism has *infinitely accelerated* this unevenness." But as for Com. Zinoviev, he in his speech at the Plenum of the E.C.C.I. considered it prudent simply to keep quiet about this question, although he could not help knowing that the dispute was precisely whether the action of the law of unevenness was intensified in the period of imperialism or weakened. But this merely evidences the fact that the discussion taught the opposition something and did not pass without being of benefit to it.

And thus: the question of the uneven development in the period of imperialism must not be confused with the question of the difference in the levels of the economic positions of the various capitalist countries.

Perhaps the lessening of the difference in the level of development of the capitalist countries and the development of the leveling process in these countries weaken the operation of the law of the uneven development under imperialism? Does this difference in the level of development increase or decrease? It undoubtedly decreases. Does the leveling process rise or fall? It undoubtedly rises. Does not the rise in the leveling process contradict the intensified unevenness of the development under capitalism? No, it does not. On the contrary, the leveling process is the background and the basis on which the intensified operation of the uneven development under capitalism is possible. Only people who do not understand the economic essence of imperialism, such as our oppositionists, can contrapose the leveling process to the law of uneven development under capitalism. Precisely because the backward countries accelerate their development and reach the level of the advanced countries – precisely for this reason the struggle of some countries to outstrip others becomes sharper, precisely for this reason *the possibility is created* for some countries to surpass other countries and to crowd them out of the markets, thereby creating the preconditions for military clashes, for weakening the world front of capitalism, for the proletarians of the various capitalist countries making a breach in this front. Whoever has not understood this simple matter has not understood anything on the question of the economic essence of monopolistic capitalism.

And thus, the leveling process is one of the conditions for intensifying the unevenness of the development in the period of imperialism.

Perhaps the uneven development under imperialism consists in the fact that some countries overtake others and then surpass them in regard to economics *in the usual way,* in the way, so to speak, of *evolution,* without leaps, without military catastrophes, without a redivision of the already divided world? No, it does not. Such an unevenness existed also in the period of pre-monopolistic capitalism, of which Marx knew and of which Lenin wrote in his *Development of Capitalism.* At that time the development of capitalism proceeded more or less smoothly, more or less by way of evolution and a few countries surpassed others during the course of a long period of time without any leaps and without the necessity of military clashes on a world scale. It is not now a question of this unevenness.

What then is the law of uneven development under imperialism?

The law of uneven development in the period of imperialism denotes the spasmodic development of some countries with reference to others, the rapid squeezing out from the world markets of some countries by others, the periodic repartitions of an *already divided world* by way of military clashes and military catastrophes, the aggravation and intensification of the conflicts in the camp of imperialism, the weakening of the front of world imperialism, the possibility of a breach in this front by the proletarians of the separate countries, the possibility of the victory of socialism in separate countries.

Wherein do the basic elements of the law of uneven development under imperialism consist?

First, in the fact that the world is already divided between imperialist groups, that there are no more "free," unoccupied territories in the world and that in order to occupy new markets and sources of raw materials and in order to expand, it has become necessary to take these territories by force.

Second, in the fact that the unprecedented development of technique and the intensified leveling process in the plane of development of the capitalist countries have created the possibility and have facilitated the spasmodic surpassing of some countries by others, the squeezing out of the more powerful countries by the less powerful but rapidly developing countries.

Third, in the fact that the old distribution of the spheres of influence between separate imperialist groups comes each time in conflict with the new correlation of forces on the world market, that for the establishment of an "equilibrium" between the old distribution of the spheres of influence and the new correlation of forces periodic redivisions of the world by means of imperialist wars are necessary.

Hence the intensification and sharpening of the uneven development in the period of imperialism.

Hence the impossibility of deciding the conflicts in the camp of imperialism by peaceful means.

Hence the untenability of the Kautskian theory of ultra-imperialism, which preaches the possibility of a peaceful solution of these conflicts.

But from this it follows that the opposition, which denies the fact that the uneven development in the period of imperialism is increased and accentuated, tumbles to the position of ultra-imperialism.

Such are the characteristic features of the uneven development in the period of imperialism.

When was the partition of the world by the imperialist groups finished?

Lenin says that the partition of the world was finished in the beginning of the twentieth century.

When was the question of the repartition of the already divided world put for the first time?

In the period of the first world imperialist war.

But from this it follows that the law of the uneven development *under imperialism* could be discovered and substantiated only in the beginning of the twentieth century.

I spoke about this in my report at the Fifteenth Conference of the All-Russian C.P., when I said that the law of the uneven development, under capitalism was discovered and substantiated by Com. Lenin.

The world imperialist war was the first attempt to repartition an already divided world. This attempt cost capitalism the victory of the revolution in Russia and the shaking of the foundations of imperialism in the colonial and dependent countries.

There is no need to state that after the first attempt at repartition a second attempt ought to follow, preparatory work for which is already going on in the camp of the imperialists.

It is hardly open to doubt that the second attempt at repartition will cost world capitalism much more than the first.

Such are the perspectives of the development of world capitalism from the point of view of the law of unevenness in the conditions of imperialism.

You see that these perspectives lead directly and indirectly to the possibility of the victory of socialism in separate capitalist countries in the period of imperialism.

It is well known that Lenin deduced the possibility of the victory of socialism in separate countries directly and indirectly from the law of the uneven development of the capitalist countries. And Lenin was absolutely right. For the law of uneven development under imperialism destroys every basis for the "theoretical exercises" of any and all socialists concerning the impossibility of the victory of socialism in separate capitalist countries.

Here is what Lenin says on this score in his programmatic article written in 1915:

> Uneven economic and political development is an absolute law of capitalism. Hence the victory of socialism is possible first in a few or even in one single capitalist country taken separately. (Lenin, "The United States of Europe Slogan," *Collected Works,* Vol. XVIII, pp. 272.)

Conclusions:

(a) The basic error of the opposition consists in the fact that it fails to see the difference between the two phases of capitalism or it evades the emphasis on this difference. And why does it evade this? Because this difference leads to the law of the uneven development in the period of imperialism.

(b) The second mistake of the opposition consists in the fact that it does not understand or underestimates the decisive importance of the law of uneven development of the capitalist countries under imperialism. And why does it underestimate this? Because a correct estimate of the law of uneven development of the capitalist countries leads to the conclusion that the victory of socialism in separate countries is possible.

(c) Hence the third mistake of the opposition, which consists in the denial of the possibility of the victory of socialism in separate capitalist countries under imperialism.

Whoever denies the possibility of the victory of socialism is compelled to pass in silence over the importance of the law of the uneven development under imperialism, and whoever is compelled to pass in silence over the law of the unevenness cannot but slur over the difference which exists between pre-imperialist capitalism and imperialist capitalism.

This is how matters stand in the question of the preconditions for the proletarian revolutions in the capitalist countries. What is the practical importance of this question?

From the point of view of practice two lines rise before us. One line is the line of our Party calling upon the proletarians of the separate countries to get ready for the oncoming revolution, to follow carefully the course of events and to be ready under favorable conditions to break the capitalist front independently, to seize power and shake the foundations of world capitalism. Another line is the line of our opposition which sows doubt concerning the expediency of an independent breach in the capitalist front and calls upon the proletarians of the separate countries to await the moment of a "general debacle."

If the line of our Party is the line for intensified revolutionary attack against one's own bourgeoisie and the unfettering of the initiative of the proletarians of the separate countries, the line of our opposition is the line of passive waiting and tying up the initiative of the proletarians of the separate countries in their struggle against their own bourgeoisie.

The first line is the line of the activization of the proletarians of the separate countries.

The second line is the line of the weakening of the will of the proletariat for revolution, the line of passivity and waiting.

Lenin was absolutely right when he wrote the following prophetic words having a direct bearing on our present disputes:

> I know that there are pundits who consider themselves very smart and even call themselves Socialists, who assert that power ought not to have been seized until the revolution had broken out in all countries. They do not suspect that in speaking thus they withdraw from the revolution and desert to the side of the bourgeoisie. To wait until the toiling classes accomplish a revolution on an international scale means that all are to grow stiff with waiting. This is nonsense.

One must not forget these words of Lenin.

Joseph Stalin, "Once More About the Social-Democratic Deviation," *On the Opposition,* 1927.

3. World System of Imperialism and the Break in the Chain of Imperialism at Its Weakest Link

Formerly, the analysis of the premises of the proletarian revolution was usually approached from the point of view of the economic situation in *any* particular country. This method is now inadequate. To-day, it must start from the point of view of the economic situation in all, or a majority of, countries – from the point of view of the state of world economy, inasmuch as the individual countries and individual national economies are no longer self-contained economic units but have become links of a single chain called world economy; inasmuch as the old "cultured" capitalism has grown into imperialism, and imperialism is a world system of financial bondage and of colonial oppression of the vast majority of the population of the globe by a handful of "advanced" countries.

Formerly, it was customary to talk of the existence or absence of objective conditions for the proletarian revolution in individual countries, or, to be more exact, in this or that advanced country. This point of view is now inadequate. Now we must say that objective conditions for the revolution exist throughout the whole system of imperialist world economy, which is an integral unit; the existence within the system of some countries that *are* not sufficiently developed from the industrial point of view cannot form an insurmountable obstacle to the revolution, *if* the system as a whole has become, or more correctly, *because* the system as a whole has already become ripe for the revolution.

Formerly, the proletarian revolution in this or that advanced country was regarded as a separate and self-contained unit, facing a separate national capitalist front, as its opposite pole. To-day this point of view is inadequate. To-day it is necessary to speak of proletarian world revolution, for the separate national fronts of capital have become links in a single chain called the world front of imperialism, to which should be opposed the united front of the revolutionary movement in all countries.

Formerly, the proletarian revolution was regarded as the consequence of an exclusively internal development in a given country. At the present time this point of view is inadequate. To-day it is necessary to regard the proletarian revolution above all as the result of the development of the contradictions within the world system of imperialism, as the result of the snapping of the chain of the imperialist world front in this or that country.

Where will the revolution begin? Where, in what country, can the front of capital be pierced first?

Formerly, the reply used to be – where industry is more developed, where the proletariat forms the majority, where culture is more advanced, where there is more democracy.

The Leninist theory of the revolution says: No, *not necessarily where industry is most developed,* and so forth; it will be broken where the chain of imperialism is weakest, for the proletarian revolution is the result of the breaking of the chain of the imperialist world front at its weakest link. The country which begins the revolution, which makes a breach in the capitalist front, may prove to be less developed in a capitalist sense than others which are more developed but have remained, nevertheless, within the framework of capitalism.

In 1917, the chain of the imperialist world front turned out to be weaker in Russia than in the other countries. It was there that it was broken and afforded an outlet for the proletarian revolution. Why? Because in Russia a very great popular revolution was being developed, led by a revolutionary proletariat, which had such an important ally as the vast mass of the peasantry who were oppressed and exploited by the landlords; because the revolution there found itself opposed by tsarism, the hideous representative of imperialism, devoid of all moral authority and deservedly hated by the whole people. The chain proved to be weakest in Russia, although that country was less developed in a capitalistic sense than, for example, France, Germany, England or America.

Where in the near future will the chain be broken next? Once more, precisely where it is weakest. It is not impossible that this may be in India, for example. Why? Because there we find a young and militant revolutionary proletariat which has an ally in the shape of the national liberation movement, unquestionably a very powerful and important ally; because in that country the revolution faces a notorious enemy, a foreign imperialism, devoid of all moral authority and deservedly hated by the oppressed and exploited masses of India.

It is just as possible that the chain will be broken in Germany. Why? Because the factors which are at work in India, for instance, are beginning to become operative in Germany as well. Of course, the tremendous difference in the level of development between India and Germany cannot but leave its impress on the progress and outcome of the revolution in Germany.

That is why Lenin said that:

> The West European capitalist countries are completing their evolution towards socialism... not by the even "maturing" of socialism in these countries, but through the exploitation of some state by others, through the exploitation of the first state that was defeated in the imperialist war in conjunction with the exploitation of the entire East. The East, on the other hand, has definitely entered the revolutionary movement as a result of this first imperialist war; it has definitely been drawn into the common whirlpool of the revolutionary movement. ("Better Less, But Better," *Collected Works,* Vol. XXVIII.)

To put it briefly, the chain of the imperialist front should break, as a rule, where the links are most fragile and, in any event, not necessarily where capitalism is most developed, or where there is a certain percentage of proletarians and a certain percentage of peasants, and so on.

This is why statistical calculations concerning the proportion of the proletariat to the population of a given country lose, in the solution of the question of the proletarian revolution, the exceptional importance so eagerly attached to them by the bookworms of the Second International who do not understand imperialism and who fear revolution like the plague.

Joseph Stalin, *Foundations of Leninism,* Chap. Ill, Section 3.

4. Lenin's Doctrine of the Weak Link and the Fight Against Bukharin's Distortion of This Doctrine

The *Pravda* of December 16 (No. 296) carried an unsigned article entitled "No Muddling, Please" (Section of "Party Structure"), where one of the propositions of an article headed "Introductory Outline of Leninism" in the *Komsomolskaya Pravda* is criticized. The proposition treats the question of the most favorable conditions for the revolutionary breach of the world imperialist front. The author cites the following quotation from the article criticized: "Leninism teaches that the revolution begins where the imperialist chain has its *weakest link.* "... The author further puts an *equal mark* between this quotation and the following quotation from Com. Bukharin's *Economics of the Transition Period:* "The collapse of the world capitalist system began with the *weakest national economic system.*" The author afterwards quotes a critical note by Lenin against the said quotation from Com. Bukharin's book[*] and infers that an error has been made in the article "Introductory Outline of Leninism" in the *Komsomolskaya Pravda* analogous to Com. Bukharin's mistake.

It seems to me that the author of the article "No Muddling, Please" has made a mistake. Under no circumstances should an *equal mark* be placed between the thesis "the imperialist chain breaks where it is weakest" and the thesis of Com. Bukharin – "the imperialist chain breaks where the national economic system is weakest." Why? Because in the first instance the reference is to the weakness of the imperialist chain *which must be broken, i.e.,* the weakness of the imperialist forces, and here, with Com. Bukharin, it is a question of the weakness of the national economic system of the country *which (i.e.,* the country) *ought to break* the chain of imperialism, *i.e.,* of the weakness of the anti-imperialist forces. That is not at all one and the same thing. Moreover, these are two opposite theses. According to Bukharin it would appear that the imperialist front breaks where the national economic system is weakest of all. This is of course not true. If this were true, the proletarian revolution would have begun somewhere in Central Africa and not in Russia. But in the article "Introductory Outline of Leninism" something *directly opposite* to the thesis of Com. Bukharin is said, namely that the imperialist chain breaks where it (the chain) is weakest. And this is absolutely correct. The chain of world imperialism breaks in a given country precisely for the reason that it (the chain) is *weakest at the given moment* precisely in that country. Otherwise it would not have broken. Otherwise the Mensheviks would have been right in their struggle against Leninism. But what determines the weakness of the imperialist chain in a given country? The presence of a certain minimum of industrial development and of culture in that country. The

---

[*] Lenin made the following notation against this quotation from Bukharin: "Wrong: from the 'fairly *weak.*' Without a certain level of capitalism nothing would have come out of it in our country." (Lenin – marginal notation, *Lenin Miscellany,* Vol. XI, "Notations on N. I. Bukharin's *Economics of the Transition Period.*) – Ed.

presence there of a certain minimum of industrial proletariat. The revolutionary spirit of the proletariat and the proletarian vanguard in that country. The presence there of a serious ally of the proletariat (the peasantry, for instance), capable of following the proletariat in the decisive struggle against imperialism. Consequently, a combination of conditions which make the isolation and the overthrow of imperialism in that country inevitable. The author of the article "No Muddling, Please" palpably confused *two absolutely different things.*

Indeed: No muddling, please.

Joseph Stalin, "Necessary Corrections," *Pravda,* December 18, 1929.

5. The Question of the Victory of Socialism in One Country in the Period of Imperialism and in the Period of Industrial Capitalism

I should further like to say a few words about the special manner in which Com. Zinoviev quotes the classics of Marxism. The characteristic feature of this manner of Zinoviev's consists in the fact that it confuses all periods and data, throws them on one pile, severs the individual postulates and formulas of Marx and Engels from their live connection with reality, converts them into time-worn dogmas and thus violates the principal demand of Marx and Engels consisting in this, that "Marxism is not a dogma but a guide to action."

Here are some facts:

1. First fact. In his speech Comrade Zinoviev quoted a certain passage from Marx's booklet *Class Struggles in France* (1848-50), which says that "the task of the working class [the point under discussion is the victory of socialism – *J. S.*] cannot be solved within the limits of national boundaries."

Com. Zinoviev further quoted the following passage from a letter by Marx to Engels (1858):

> The difficult question for us is this: on the Continent the revolution is imminent and will also immediately assume a socialist character. Is it not bound to be crushed in this little corner, considering that in a far greater territory the movement of bourgeois society is still on the ascendent? (Letter of October 8, 1858; see *The Corre-*

spondence of Marx and Engels, p. 118.)

Comrade Zinoviev quotes these passages from Marx written during the forties and fifties of the last century and arrives at the conclusion that thereby the question of the victory of socialism in separate countries has been decided in the negative *for all times and periods of capitalism.*

Can it be said that Comrade Zinoviev understood Marx, his point of view, his basic line on the question of the victory of socialism in separate countries? No, this cannot be said. On the contrary, from these quotations it is apparent that Comrade Zinoviev entirely misunderstood Marx, that he distorted the basic viewpoint of Marx.

Does it follow from the quotation from Marx that the victory of socialism is impossible under *all* conditions of development of capitalism? No, it does not. From Marx's words it merely follows that the victory of socialism in separate countries is impossible only in the event that the "movement of bourgeois society is still on the ascendent." Well, and what if the movement of bourgeois society as a whole by virtue of the course of events changes its direction and begins to proceed in a *descending* line? From Marx's words it follows that under *such* conditions the basis for the denial of the possibility of the victory of socialism in separate countries disappears.

Com. Zinoviev forgets that the quotations from Marx refer to the period of pre-monopolistic capitalism, when capitalism as a whole was developing in an ascending line, when the growth of capitalism as a whole was not accompanied by the process of decay of capitalistically so developed a country as England, when the law of the uneven development did not yet represent, and could not represent, so powerful a factor in the decay of capitalism as it became later on, in the period of monopolistic capitalism, in the period of imperialism. For the period of pre-monopolistic capitalism the words of Marx to the effect that the solution of the basic problem of the working class is impossible in separate countries are absolutely correct. Already in my report at the Fifteenth Conference of C.P.S.U. I said that for the old times, for the period of pre-monopolistic capitalism, the question of the victory of socialism in separate countries was decided in the negative and absolutely correctly so. Well, but now, in the present period of capitalism, when pre-monopolistic capitalism has grown into imperialistic capitalism, can it be said that capitalism as a whole is developing in an ascending line? No, it cannot. The analysis of the economic essence of imperialism made by Lenin indicates that in the period of imperialism bourgeois society as a whole proceeds in a descending line. Lenin is absolutely right when he says that monopolistic capitalism, imperialistic capitalism, is *moribund* capitalism. Here is what Comrade Lenin says on this score:

> It is clear why imperialism is *moribund* capitalism, the *transition* to socialism: monopoly growing *out* of capitalism is *already* the dying out of capitalism, the beginning of its transition to socialism. The tremendous *socialization* of labor by imperialism (what the apologetic bourgeois economists call "interlocking") signifies the same thing. (Lenin, "Imperialism and the Split in the Socialist Movement," *Collected Works,* Vol. XIX.)

Pre-monopolistic capitalism, developing as a whole in an ascending line, is one thing. Imperialistic capitalism, when the world has already been divided among the capitalist groups, when the spasmodic development of capitalism demands new re-divisions of an already divided world by means of military clashes, when the conflicts and wars among the imperialist groups which arise on this ground weaken the world front of imperialism, render it easily vulnerable and create the possibility of a breach in this front in the separate countries, is another thing. There, under pre-monopolistic capitalism, the victory of socialism in separate countries was regarded as impossible. Here, in the period of imperialism, in the period of moribund capitalism, the victory of socialism in separate countries has already become possible.

This is the point, Comrades, and this is what Comrade Zinoviev does not want to understand.

You see that Comrade Zinoviev quotes Marx like a schoolboy who, while turning away from Marx's *viewpoint* and seizing upon isolated quotations from Marx, applies these same quotations not like a Marxist but like a Social-Democrat.

Wherein consists the revisionist manner of quoting Marx? The revisionist manner of quoting Marx consists in substituting for Marx's *viewpoint quotations* from separate postulates of Marx taken in disregard of the concrete conditions of the definite epoch with which they are connected.

Wherein consists the Zinoviev manner of quoting Marx? The

Zinoviev manner of quoting Marx consists in substituting for Marx's *viewpoint,* the letter, *quotations* from Marx severed from live contact with the conditions of development of the fifties of the nineteenth century and converted into a dogma.

Joseph Stalin, "Once More on the Social-Democratic Deviation in Our Party," *On the Opposition.*

6. The Victory of the Revolution in One Country as an Aid and Instrument for Accelerating the Victory of the Proletariat in All Countries

There is no doubt that the universal theory of the simultaneous victory of revolution in the principal countries of Europe, the theory that the victory of socialism in one country is impossible, has turned out to be an artificial and untenable theory. The seven years' history of the proletarian revolution in Russia speaks not for but against this theory. This theory is inacceptable not only as a scheme of development of the world revolution, for it is in contradiction to obvious facts. It is still less acceptable as a slogan, for it fetters rather than releases the initiative of different countries which, by force of certain historical conditions, are given the opportunity by their own efforts to break through the front of capital, for it does not stimulate an active attack on capital in separate countries, but inculcates passive waiting for the moment of the "universal climax"; for among the proletarians of the different countries it cultivates, not the spirit of revolutionary determination, but the mood of Hamletian doubt as to whether "the others will back us up." Lenin was absolutely right in saying that the victory of the proletariat in a single country forms a "typical case," that the "simultaneous revolution in a number of countries" can be only a "rare exception." (*Cf. Proletarian Revolution and Renegade Kautsky,* 1918.)

But, as is well known, Lenin's theory of revolution is not limited to this one side of the matter. It is at the same time a theory of the development of the world revolution. The victory of socialism in one country is not a self-sufficient task. In the country where it is victorious the revolution must regard itself, not as a self-sufficient quantity, but as a support, a means for hastening the victory of the proletariat in all countries. For the victory of the revolution in one single country, in this case Russia, is not only a product of the uneven development and progressive decay of imperialism. It constitutes at the same time the beginning and premise of the world revolution.

Beyond a doubt, the way of development of the world revolution is not so simple as it may once have seemed before the victory of socialism in one country, before the appearance of highly developed imperialism, which represents the "eve of the socialist revolution." For a new factor had arisen, *viz.,* the law of the uneven development of the capitalist countries, which operates under the conditions of developed imperialism and which connotes the inevitability of military collisions, of the general weakening of the world front of capital and of the possibility of the victory of socialism in separate countries. For a new factor has arisen, *viz.,* the huge Soviet country, lying between West and East, between the center of financial exploitation of the world and the area of colonial oppression, a country which by its very existence is revolutionizing the entire world.

All these are factors (I do not mention other less important factors) which cannot be left out of account in studying the path of development of the world revolution.

Formerly it was commonly thought that the revolution would develop through the even "ripening" of the elements of socialism, especially in the more developed, the more "advanced" countries. At the present time this view must be considerably modified.

> The system of international relationships – says Lenin – has now become such that in Europe one state, namely, Germany, has been enslaved by the victorious states. Next, a number of states, including the oldest states of the West, have proved, as a result of their victory, to be in a position to take advantage of this victory to make a number of unimportant concessions to their oppressed classes, concessions which nevertheless delay the revolutionary movement in those countries and create some semblance of "social peace."
>
> At the same time a whole series of countries, the Orient, India, China, etc., by reason of the last imperialist war, have proved to be definitely thrown out of their orbits. Their development has once and for all been directed along the general European and capitalist path. The general European ferment has begun to work in them. And it is now clear to the entire world that they have been drawn into a

line of development which cannot help but lead to the crisis of world capitalism.

In view of this fact and in connection with it the West European capitalist countries are completing their evolution towards socialism... not by the even "maturing" of socialism in these countries, but through the exploitation of some states by others, through the exploitation of the first state that was defeated in the imperialist war in conjunction with the exploitation of the entire East. The East, on the other hand, has definitely entered the revolutionary movement as a result of this first imperialist war; it has definitely been drawn into the common whirlpool of the revolutionary movement. (Lenin, "Better Less, But Better," *Collected Works,* Vol. XXVII.)

If we add to this the fact that not only the defeated countries and colonies are being exploited by the victorious countries, but that some of the victorious countries have fallen into the orbit of financial exploitation by the more powerful of the victorious powers, America and England; that the contradictions among all these countries form a very important factor in the decay of world capitalism; that in addition to these contradictions very profound contradictions exist and are developing within each one of these countries; that all these contradictions are growing in profundity and acuteness because of the existence, alongside these countries, of the Republic of Soviets – if all this is taken into consideration, then the picture of the peculiar nature of the international situation becomes more or less complete.

Most probably, the world revolution will develop along the line of a series of new countries dropping out of the system of the imperialist countries as a result of revolution, while the proletarians of these countries will be supported by the proletariat of the imperialist states. We see that the first country to break away, the first country to win, is already supported by the workers and toiling masses of other countries. Without this support it could not maintain itself. Beyond a doubt, this support will grow and become stronger and stronger. But it is likewise beyond a doubt that the very development of the world revolution, the very process of the breaking away of a number of new countries from imperialism, will be more rapid and more thorough, the more thoroughly socialism fortifies itself in the first victorious country, the faster this country is transformed into the basis for the further unfolding of the world revolution, into the lever for the further disintegration of imperialism.

If the postulate that the *final* victory of socialism in the first country to emancipate itself is impossible without the combined efforts of the proletarians of several countries is true, then it is just as true that the world revolution will develop the more rapidly and thoroughly, the more effective the assistance rendered by the first socialist country to the workers and toiling masses of all other countries will be.

By what should this assistance be expressed?

It should be expressed, first, by the victorious country achieving "the utmost possible in one country for the development, support and stirring up of the revolution *in all countries.*" (*Proletarian Revolution and Renegade Kautsky,* Chap. VII, "What Is Internationalism?")

Second, it should be expressed by the "victorious proletariat" of one country, "after it has expropriated the capitalists and organized its socialist production at home, rising... against the rest of the capitalist world, attracting to itself the oppressed classes of other countries, raising insurrection in them against the capitalists, acting in case of need even with military force against the exploiting classes and their states." ("The United States of Europe Slogan," *Collected Works,* Vol. XVIII.)

The characteristic feature of the assistance given by the victorious country is that it not only hastens the victory of the proletarians of other countries, but likewise guarantees, by facilitating this victory, the *final* victory of socialism in the first victorious country.

The most probable thing is that, side by side with the centers of imperialism in separate capitalist countries and in the systems of these countries throughout the world, centers of socialism will be created, in the course of the world revolution, in separate soviet countries and systems of these centers throughout the world, and the struggle between these two systems will constitute the history of the development of the revolution:

> For – says Lenin – the free amalgamation of nations in socialism is impossible without a more or less prolonged and stubborn struggle by the socialist republics against the backward states. (*Ibid.*)

The world significance of the October Revolution lies not only in its constituting a start made by one country in the work of breaking through the system of imperialism and the creation of the first land of socialism in the ocean of imperialist countries, but likewise in its constituting the first stage in the world revolution and a mighty basis for its further development.

Therefore, those who, forgetting the international character of the October Revolution, declare the victory of socialism in one country to be purely national and only a national phenomenon, are wrong. And those too who, although bearing in mind the international character of the October Revolution, are inclined to regard this revolution as something passive, merely destined to accept help from without, are equally wrong. As a matter of fact not only does the October Revolution need support from the revolutionary movement of other countries, but revolution in those countries needs the support of the October Revolution in order to accelerate and advance the cause of overthrowing world imperialism.

Joseph Stalin, "The Tactics of the Russian Communists," *The October Revolution,* pp. 122-129.

III. MAIN TYPES OF REVOLUTION IN THE EPOCH OF IMPERIALISM AND THE GROWING OF THE BOURGEOIS DEMOCRATIC REVOLUTION INTO THE PROLETARIAN REVOLUTION

1. Struggle for the Dictatorship of the Proletariat and the Main Types of Revolution

The international proletarian revolution represents a combination of processes which vary in time and character: purely proletarian revolutions; revolutions of a bourgeois-democratic type which grow into proletarian revolutions; wars for national liberation; colonial revolutions. The world dictatorship of the proletariat comes only as the final result of the revolutionary process.

The uneven development of capitalism, which became more accentuated in the period of imperialism, has given rise to a variety of types of capitalism, to different stages of ripeness of capitalism in different countries, and to a variety of specific conditions of the revolutionary process. These circumstances make it historically inevitable that the proletariat will come to power by a variety of ways and degrees of rapidity; that a number of countries must pass through certain transition stages leading to the dictatorship of the proletariat and must adopt varied forms of socialist construction.

The variety of conditions and ways by which the proletariat will achieve its dictatorship in the various countries may be divided schematically into three main types.

Countries of highly-developed capitalism (United States of America, Germany, Great Britain, etc.), having powerful productive forces, highly centralized production, with small scale production reduced to relative insignificance, and a long established bourgeois-democratic political system. In such countries the fundamental political demand of the program is direct transition to the dictatorship of the proletariat. In the economic sphere, the most characteristic demands are: expropriation of the whole of large-scale industry; organization of a large number of state Soviet farms and, in contrast to this, a relatively small portion of the land to be transferred to the peasantry; unregulated market relations to be given comparatively small scope; rapid rate of socialist development generally, and of collectivization of peasant farming in particular.

Countries with a medium development of capitalism (Spain,

Portugal, Poland, Hungary, the Balkan countries, etc.), having numerous survivals of semi-feudal relationships in agriculture, possessing, to a certain extent, the material prerequisites for socialist construction, and in which the bourgeois-democratic reforms have not yet been completed. In some of these countries a process of more or less rapid development from bourgeois-democratic revolution to socialist revolution is possible. In others, there may be types of proletarian revolution which will have a large number of bourgeois-democratic tasks to fulfill, Hence, in these countries, the dictatorship of the proletariat may not come about at once, but in the process of transition from the democratic dictatorship of the proletariat and peasantry to the socialist dictatorship of the proletariat; where the revolution develops directly as a proletarian revolution it is presumed that the proletariat exercises leadership over a broad agrarian peasant movement. In general, the agrarian revolution plays a most important part in these countries, and in some cases a decisive role; in the process of expropriating large landed property a considerable portion of the confiscated land is placed at the disposal of the peasantry; the volume of market relations prevailing after the victory of the proletariat is considerable; the task of organizing the peasantry along cooperative lines and later, of combining them in production, occupies an important place among the tasks of socialist construction. The rate of this construction is relatively slow.

Colonial and semi-colonial countries (China, India, etc.) and dependent countries (Argentine, Brazil, etc.), having the rudiments of and in some cases considerably developed industry, but in the majority of cases inadequate for independent socialist construction; with feudal medieval relationships, or "Asiatic mode of production" relationships prevailing in their economies and in their political superstructures; and in which the principal industrial, commercial and banking enterprises, the principal means of transport, the large landed estates (latifundia), plantations, etc., are concentrated in the hands of foreign imperialist groups. The principal task in such countries is, on the one hand, to fight against the feudalism and the precapitalist forms of exploitation and to systematically develop the peasant agrarian revolution; on the other hand, to fight against foreign imperialism for national independence. As a rule, transition to the dictatorship of the proletariat in these countries will be possible only through a series of preparatory stages, as the outcome of a whole period of transformation of bourgeois-democratic revolution into socialist revolution, while in the majority of cases, successful socialist construction will be possible only if direct support is obtained from the countries in which the proletarian dictatorship is established.

In still more backward countries (as in some parts of Africa) where there are no wage workers or very few, where the majority of the population still live in tribal conditions, where survivals of primitive tribal forms still exist, where the national bourgeoisie is almost non-existent, where the primary role of foreign imperialism is that of military occupation and usurpation of land, the central task is to fight for national independence. Victorious national uprisings in these countries may open the way for their direct development towards socialism and their avoiding the stage of capitalism, provided real, powerful assistance is rendered to them by the countries in which the proletarian dictatorship is established.

Thus, in the epoch in which the proletariat in the most developed capitalist countries is confronted with the immediate task of capturing power, in which the dictatorship of the proletariat is already established in the U.S.S.R. and is a factor of world significance, the movement for liberation in colonial and semi-colonial countries, which was brought into being by the penetration of world capitalism, may lead to *socialist development* – notwithstanding the immaturity of social relationships in these countries taken by themselves – *provided they receive the assistance and support of the proletarian dictatorship and of the international proletarian movement generally.*

Program of the Communist International, Part IV, Section 8.

2. The Growing of the Bourgeois-Democratic Revolution Into the Socialist Revolution

A. Stalin on the Growing of the Bourgeois-Democratic Revolution into the Proletarian Revolution and on the Anti-Marxian Nature of the Trotskyist Theory of Permanent Revolution

To proceed: The heroes of the Second International asserted (and keep on asserting) that between the bourgeois-democratic revolution and the proletarian revolution there is a chasm, or at any rate a Chinese Wall, separating one from the other by a period of time more or less protracted, in the course of which the bourgeoisie, having come into power, develops capitalism, while the proletariat accumulates forces and prepares for the "decisive struggle" against capitalism. This interval is supposed to extend over many decades, if not longer. That this Chinese Wall "theory" is totally devoid of scientific meaning under imperialism hardly needs to be proved; it is and can be only a means of concealing and camouflaging the counter-revolutionary aspirations of the bourgeoisie. It need hardly be proved that under the conditions of imperialism, which is pregnant with collisions and wars, under the conditions prevailing on the "eve of the socialist revolution," when "flourishing" capitalism is becoming "moribund" capitalism, and when the revolutionary movement is growing in every country in the world, when imperialism is allying itself with all reactionary forces without exception down to and including tsarism and serfdom, thus making the coalition of all revolutionary forces, from the proletarian movement of the West to the national liberation movement of the East, imperative, when the overthrow of the survivals of the feudal-serf regime becomes impossible without a revolutionary struggle against imperialism – it need hardly be proved that the bourgeois-democratic revolution, in a country more or less developed, should under such circumstances approximate to the proletarian revolution, that the one should grow into the other. The history of the revolution in Russia has given palpable proof of the correctness and incontrovertibility of this postulate. It was not for nothing that Lenin, as far back as 1905, on the eve of the first Russian revolution (in his pamphlet, *Two Tactics of Social-Democracy in the Bourgeois-Democratic Revolution*), depicted the bourgeois-democratic revolution and the socialist revolution as two links in the same chain, as a single and complete picture of the sweep of the Russian revolution:

> The proletariat must carry out to the end the democratic revolution, and in this unite to itself the mass of the peasantry in order to crush by force the resistance of the autocracy and to paralyze the instability of the bourgeoisie. The proletariat must accomplish the socialist revolution and in this unite to itself the mass of the semi-proletarian elements of the population in order to crush by force the resistance of the bourgeoisie and to paralyze the instability of the peasantry and petty bourgeoisie. Such are the tasks of the proletariat, which the new *Iskra-ists* in their arguments and resolutions about the sweep of the revolution present in such a narrow manner. (V. I. Lenin, *Two Tactics of Social-*

Democracy in the Bourgeois-Democratic Revolution, Chap. XII, Little Lenin Library, Vol. 22.)

I shall not speak here of other and later works of Lenin in which the idea of the bourgeois revolution growing into the proletarian revolution is set forth still more emphatically than in *Two Tactics* as one of the cornerstones of the Leninist theory of revolution.

It turns out that certain comrades believe that this idea occurred to Lenin only in 1916 and that previously he thought that the revolution in Russia would remain within a bourgeois framework and that power, consequently, would pass from the hands of the organ of the dictatorship of the proletariat and peasantry to the hands of the bourgeoisie and not of the proletariat. This assertion has, it is said, even penetrated into our Communist press. But I am bound to say that this assertion is absolutely incorrect and is absolutely at variance with the facts.

I might refer to Lenin's well-known speech at the Third Party Congress (1905), in which Lenin termed the dictatorship of the proletariat and peasantry, that is to say, the victory of the democratic revolution, not the "organization of order" but the "organization of war" (*Collected Works,* Vol. VII, p. 264).

Further, I could recall Lenin's well-known article *On the Provisional Government* (1905), in which Lenin, depicting the prospects of development of the revolution in Russia, assigns to the Party the task of "striving to make the Russian revolution not a movement of a few months but of many years, so that it may lead, not merely to slight concessions on the part of the powers that be, but to the complete overthrow of these authorities," where, developing further the picture of this revolution, which he connects with that of Europe, Lenin goes on to say:

> And if we succeed... the revolutionary conflagration will spread all over Europe; the European worker, languishing under bourgeois reaction, will rise in his turn and will show us "how the thing is done"; then the revolutionary wave in Europe will sweep back again into Russia and will convert an epoch of a few revolutionary years into an era of several revolutionary decades ("Social-Democracy and Provisional Revolutionary Government" *Selected Works,* Vol. III).

I could also cite the well-known article published in November,

1915, in which Lenin writes:

> The proletariat is fighting, and will valiantly fight, for the conquest of power, for a republic, for land confiscation... for the participation of the "non-proletarian peoples' masses" in freeing *bourgeois* Russia from *military-feudal* imperialism (tsarism). This liberation of bourgeois Russia from tsarism, from the land power of the landowners, the proletariat will *immediately* [Emphasis mine. – *J. S.*] utilize not to aid the prosperous peasants in their struggle against the village worker, but to complete a socialist revolution in alliance with the proletarians of Europe. ("Two Lines of the Revolution," *Collected Works,* Vol. XVIII, p. 363.)

Finally, I could refer to a well-known passage from *The Proletarian Revolution and Renegade Kautsky* where Lenin, referring to the aforementioned quotation from *Two Tactics* about the scope of the Russian revolution, arrives at the following conclusion:

> Things have turned out just as we said they would. The course taken by the revolution has confirmed the correctness of our reasoning. *First,* with "all" the peasantry against the monarchy, the landlords, the medieval regime (and to that extent, the revolution remains bourgeois, bourgeois-democratic). *Then,* with the poorest peasants, with the semi-proletarians, with all the exploited, *against capitalism,* including the rural rich, the kulaks, the speculators, and to that extent the revolution becomes a *socialist* one. To attempt to raise an artificial Chinese Wall between the first and second revolutions, to separate them by anything else than the degree of preparedness of the proletariat and the degree of unity with the poor peasants, is to seriously distort Marxism, to vulgarize it, to substitute liberalism in its stead. (*The Proletarian Revolution and Renegade Kautsky,* Chap. VIII.)

This is enough, I think. But we are told, if that is so, why did Lenin oppose the idea of the "permanent (uninterrupted) revolution"?

Because Lenin proposed that the revolutionary capacities of the peasantry be utilized "to the utmost" and that full use be made of their revolutionary energy for the complete liquidation of tsarism and the transition to the proletarian revolution; whereas the adherents of "permanent revolution" did not understand the important role of the peasantry in the Russian revolution, underestimated the revolutionary energy of the peasantry, underestimated the strength and capacity of the Russian proletariat to lead the peasantry, and so hampered the work of emancipating the peasantry from the influence of the bourgeoisie, the work of rallying the peasantry around the proletariat.

Because Lenin proposed to *crown* the revolution with the coming into power of the proletariat, while the adherents of "permanent" revolution wanted to *begin* at once by establishing the power of the proletariat, not realizing that by so doing they were closing their eyes to such "trifles" as the existence of survivals of serfdom and overlooking, in their calculations, so important a force as the Russian peasantry, nor did they realize that this policy would retard the winning over of the peasantry to the side of the proletariat.

Lenin, then, fought the adherents of "permanent" revolution not over the question of "uninterruptedness," because he himself held the point of view of uninterrupted revolution, but because they underestimated the role of the peasantry, the proletariat's greatest reserve power, and because they failed to grasp the idea of the hegemony of the proletariat.

The idea of "permanent" revolution is not new. It was propounded for the first time by Marx at the end of the forties in his well-known *Address to the Communist League* (1850). This document is the source from which our "permanentists" derived the idea of uninterrupted revolution. It should be noted, however, that, in taking it from Marx, our "permanentists" slightly alter it and in altering it "spoiled" it and made it unfit for practical use. The skillful hand of Lenin was needed to correct this error, to bring out Marx's idea of uninterrupted revolution in its pure form and make it a cornerstone of his theory of the revolution.

This is what Marx says in regard to uninterrupted revolution in his *Address*. After enumerating a number of the revolutionary-democratic demands which he called upon the Communists to win, he says:

> While the democratic petty bourgeois wish to bring the revolution to a conclusion as quickly as possible, and with the achievement, at most, of the above demands, it is our

interest and our task to make the revolution permanent, until all more or less possessing classes have been displaced from domination, until the proletariat has conquered state power and the association of proletarians, not only in one country but in all the dominant countries of the world, has advanced so far that competition among the proletarians of these countries has ceased and that at least the decisive productive forces are concentrated in the hands of the proletarians.

In other words:

(a) The plan of our "permanentists" *notwithstanding,* Marx did not at all propose to *begin* the revolution in the Germany of the fifties with the direct establishment of the proletarian power.

(b) Marx proposed the establishment of proletarian political power merely as the *crowning event* of the revolution, after hurling step by step one section of the bourgeoisie after another from its height of power, in order to ignite the torch of revolution in every country after the proletariat had come to power. Now this is *perfectly consistent* with all that Lenin taught, with all that he did in the course of our revolution in pursuit of his theory of the proletarian revolution in an imperialist environment.

It turns out that our Russian "permanentists" have not only underestimated the role of the peasantry in the Russian revolution and the importance of the conception of the hegemony of the proletariat, but have modified (for the worse) the Marxian idea of "permanent" revolution and deprived it of all practical value.

That is why Lenin ridiculed their theory, ironically calling it "original" and "splendid," and accused them of refusing to "think why life, during a whole decade, has passed by this beautiful theory." (Lenin's article was written in 1915, ten years after the appearance of the theory of the "permanentists" in Russia.) (*Collected Works,* Vol. XVIII, p. 362.)

That is why he thought this theory was semi-Menshevik and said that it "takes from the Bolsheviks their appeal to decisive revolutionary struggle of the proletariat and to the conquest of political power by it; from the Mensheviks it takes the negation of the role of the peasantry." (*ibid.*)

This, then, is how Lenin conceived the growth of the bourgeois-democratic revolution into the proletarian revolution and the utilization of the bourgeois revolution for the "immediate" transition to the proletarian revolution.

Joseph Stalin, *Foundations of Leninism,* Chap. Ill, Section 3.

B. Marx and Engels on the Growing of the Bourgeois Democratic Revolution into the Proletarian Revolution

The relationship of the revolutionary workers' party to petty-bourgeois democracy is as follows: it marches side by side with it against the fraction whose overthrow it aims at; it opposes them in everything whereby they want to get a footing for themselves.

The democratic petty bourgeoisie is far from desiring to transform the whole of society for the revolutionary proletarians, strive for a change of social conditions, whereby existing society will be made as tolerable and comfortable as possible for them. They therefore demand above all a retrenchment in the expenditures of the state through a curtailment of the bureaucracy and a shift of the principal taxes on to the big landlords and bourgeois. They further demand the removal of the pressure of big capital upon small capital through public credit institutions and laws against usury whereby they and the peasants are enabled to receive advances from the state instead of from the capitalists and on advantageous terms; furthermore the carrying out of bourgeois property relationships in the countryside through the complete abolition of feudalism. In order to carry out all this they need a democratic, either monarchical or republican constitution which gives them and their allies, the peasants, a majority, and a democratic municipal code which will deliver into their hands the direct control of the municipal property and a number of functions which are now being exercised by the bureaucrats.

The domination and rapid increase of capital is further to be counteracted partly by limiting the right of inheritance, partly by transferring as many jobs as possible to the state. As regards the workers, it is certain above all that they are to remain wage slaves as heretofore. The democratic petty bourgeois only desire wages and security of existence for the workers and hope to achieve this through partial employment on the part of the state and through charity measures; in brief, they hope to bribe the workers through more or less concealed aims and to break their revolutionary power by making their position bearable for the moment. The demands of petty bourgeois democracy which have here been summarized are not presented by all its fractions at the same time and in their entirety only the fewest of their people have them before their eyes as a definite goal. The further individual persons or fractions among them go, the more of these demands they will make their own, and the few who see their own program in what has been stated before would believe that they have thereby set forth the utmost that is to be expected from the revolution. But these demands cannot satisfy the party of the proletariat by any means. While the democratic petty bourgeois wish to bring the revolution to a conclusion as quickly as possible and with the achievements at most of the above demands it is our interest and our task to make the revolution permanent, until all more or less possessing classes have been displaced from domination, until the proletariat has conquered state power and the association of proletarians, not only in one country but in all the dominated countries of the world, has advanced so far that competition among the proletarians of these countries has ceased and that at least the decisive productive forces are concentrated in the hands of the proletarians. For us there can be no talk of a transformation of private property, but only of its destruction, not of a slurring over of the class contradictions but of the abolition of classes, not of an improvement of existing society but of founding a new one. That petty bourgeois democracy during the further development of the revolution will for a moment receive the predominant influence in Germany is not open to any doubt. The question therefore is what the position of the proletariat and especially of the League will be with reference to petty-bourgeois democracy:

(1) During the continuance of the present conditions when the petty-bourgeois democrats are likewise oppressed?

(2) In the next revolutionary struggle which will make them preponderant?

(3) After this struggle, while it is preponderant over the overthrown classes and the proletariat?

1. At the present moment, when the petty bourgeois are everywhere oppressed, they in general preach to the proletariat harmony and conciliation; they offer them their hands and strive to establish a grand opposition party which will embrace every hue in the democratic party, *i.e.,* they aim to enmesh the workers in a party organization in which the general social-democratic phrases will be predominant, behind which their special interests will be concealed and in which the definite demands of the proletariat dare not be ad-

vanced for the sake of peace. Such a union would eventuate solely to their advantage and entirely to the disadvantage of the proletariat. The proletariat would lose its entire independent position which it has bought at such pains and would again sink down to the condition of an appendage of official bourgeois democracy. This union must therefore be rejected most determinedly. Instead of degrading themselves once more by acting as the applauding gallery for the bourgeois democrats, the Workers, especially the League, must exert themselves to set up alongside of the official democrats an independent, secret and public organization of the workers' party and to make every community a center and nucleus of workers' societies, in which the position and interests of the proletariat are discussed independently of the bourgeois influences. How little the bourgeois democrats take seriously this alliance in which the proletarians are arranged alongside of them with equal power and equal rights is shown for instance by the Breslau democrats who in their organ, the *Neue Oderzeitung,* fiercely attack the independently organized workers whom they give the appellation of socialists. For the event of a struggle against a common opponent no special union is needed. As soon as such an opponent is to be fought directly, the interests of both parties for the moment coincide and as heretofore so hereafter this association calculated only for the moment will arise of itself. It goes without saying that in the impending bloody conflicts as in all preceding ones the workers will have to gain the victory chiefly by their courage, decision and self-sacrifice. As before so also in this struggle, the bulk of the petty bourgeoisie will waver, vacillate and remain inactive as long as possible, only to sequester the victory for itself as soon as it has been gained, to urge the workers to be calm and to return to their work, to prevent so-called excesses and to exclude the proletariat from the fruits of victory. It does not lie in the power of the workers to prohibit the petty-bourgeois democrats from doing this, but it does lie in their power to render their advance as against the armed proletariat more difficult and to dictate to them such conditions that the domination of the bourgeois democrats will in advance harbor the germ of decline and will considerably facilitate its subsequent replacement by the domination of the proletariat. During the conflict and immediately after the struggle, the workers must above all and as far as at all possible counteract the bourgeois appeasement and force the democrats to carry into life their present terrorist phrases. They must work to the end that the immediate revolutionary agitation be not suppressed again right after the victory. They must on the contrary maintain it as long as possible. Far from opposing the so-called excesses, the examples of popular vengeance taken on hated individuals or public buildings with which only invidious memories are connected, these examples must not only be tolerated but leadership itself over them must be assumed. During the struggle and after the struggle the workers must at every opportunity set forth their own demands alongside of those of the bourgeois democrats. They must demand guarantees for the workers as soon as the democratic burghers get ready to take the government into their own hands. If necessary they must obtain these guarantees by force and in general must see to it that the new rulers pledge themselves to every possible concession and promise – the surest way of compromising them. In general they must restrain in every way the intoxication of victory and the enthusiasm for the new state of affairs which arises each time after victorious street fighting by a calm and cool-headed comprehension of conditions and by unconcealed distrust of the new government. Alongside of the new official governments they must at the same time establish their own revolutionary workers' governments, either in the form of municipal executive committees, municipal councils, or through workers' clubs or workers' committees, so that the bourgeois democratic governments not only immediately lose their support among the workers but see at the very start that they are supervised and threatened by authorities which are backed by the entire mass of the workers. In a word: from the first moment of victory, their distrust must no longer be directed against the defeated reactionary party but against their former allies, against the party that wants to exploit the common victory alone.

2. However, in order to be able energetically and threateningly to oppose this party, whose betrayal of the workers will commence from the first hour of victory, the workers must be armed and organized. The arming of the entire proletariat with shot-guns, muskets, heavy guns and ammunition must immediately be carried through; the revival of the old civil militia, directed against the workers, must be opposed. Where the latter cannot be carried through, the workers must try to organize independently as a proletarian guard, with a commander chosen by themselves and their own general staff chosen by themselves and to come under the command not of the state power but of the revolutionary municipal councils that have suc-

ceeded in installing the workers. Where the workers are employed for the account of the state, they must carry through their arming and organization either in a separate corps with commanders chosen by themselves or as part of the proletarian guard. Under no pretext may they let the arms and ammunition out of their possession; every attempt to disarm them must if necessary be frustrated by force. The destruction of the influence of the bourgeois democrats upon the workers, the immediate independent and armed organization of the workers and the carrying through of the most onerous and most compromising conditions possible for the momentary inevitable rule of bourgeois democracy – these are the main points which the proletariat and hence the League must bear in mind during and after the impending uprising.

3. As soon as the new governments have become somewhat consolidated, their struggle against the workers will immediately begin. In order to be able here to offer powerful opposition to the democratic petty bourgeoisie, it is necessary above all that the workers be organized and centralized independently in clubs. As soon as this is at all possible, the central board will remove to Germany after the fall of the existing governments, will immediately convene a congress and submit to it the necessary proposals concerning the centralization of the workers' clubs under a management established at the principal seat of the movement. Rapid organization, at least a provincial interlinking of the workers' clubs, is one of the chief points for strengthening and developing the workers' party: the immediate consequences of the overthrow of the existing government will be the election of a national assembly. Here the proletariat must see to it:

1. That no group of workers be excluded under any pretext by any chicanery on the part of local authorities or government commissars.

2. That alongside the bourgeois-democratic candidates, workers' candidates be put up everywhere, which must consist as far as possible of members of the League and whose election is to be promoted by every possible means. Even where there is absolutely no prospect of carrying the election the workers must set up their own candidates in order to preserve their independence, to count their forces, to bring their revolutionary position and the party point of view before the public. In doing so they must not allow themselves to be bribed by the locutions of the democrats, as for instance

that thereby the democratic party was being split and reaction was being given the possibility of victory. In the long run all these phrases simply amount to this, that the proletariat is to be hoodwinked. The progress which the proletarian Party must make by thus moving independently is infinitely more important than the disadvantage that could arise from the presence of a few reactionaries in the convention. If the democrats at the very outset take a decided and terroristic stand against the reactionaries, the influence of the latter at the elections is destroyed in advance.

The first point where the bourgeois democrats will come in conflict with the workers will be the abolition of feudalism; as in the first French Revolution,[*] the petty bourgeoisie will give the feudal lands to the peasants as free property, *i.e.,* they will allow the rural proletariat to remain and will want to form a petty-bourgeois peasant class which will pass through the same cycle of impoverishment and indebtedness as that in which the French peasant still finds himself.

In the interests of the rural proletariat and in their own interests the workers must oppose this plan. They must demand that the confiscated property remain public property and be used for workers' colonies which the organized rural proletariat will till with all the advantages of large-scale agriculture and whereby the principle of common property will immediately receive a firm foundation in the midst of the tottering bourgeois property relations. As the democrats unite with the peasants, so the workers must unite with the rural proletariat. Furthermore, the democrats will either work directly for a federative republic, or, if they cannot avoid a single inseparable republic, they will seek to paralyze the central government through the greatest possible autonomy and independence of the municipalities and provinces. As against this plan the workers must exert themselves not only in favor of one inseparable German republic but also of the most decided centralization of power in it in the hands of the state power. They must not permit themselves to be misled by democratic talk of the freedom of municipalities, of home rule, etc. In a country like Germany where so many remnants of the Middle Ages are to be removed, where so much local and provincial obstinacy is to be broken, it must not under any circumstances be tolerated that each village, each town, each province place a new

---

[*] The Great French Revolution which began in 1789. – *Ed.*

obstacle in the path of the revolutionary activity which can proceed in its entire strength only from the center. It is not to be tolerated that present conditions be renewed under which the Germans must fight a separate battle in each town, in each province, for one and the same progress. Least of all may it be tolerated that a form of property which is still behind modern private property and everywhere necessarily resolved itself into this, perpetuate, through a so-called free municipal code, municipal property and the disputes which arise from this between the poor and the rich municipalities, as well as the municipal civil law with its chicanery against the workers existing alongside of the state civil law. Just as in France in 1793 so to-day in Germany it is the task of a really revolutionary party to carry through the strictest centralization.*

We have seen how the democrats in the next movement come into power, how they will be compelled to propose more or less socialist measures. The question may be put: What measures are the workers to propose against this? Of course the workers cannot at the beginning of the movement propose any directly communist

---

* To-day one must call to mind that this passage is based on a misapprehension. At that time it was taken for granted – owing to the Bonapartist and liberal forgers of history – that the French centralized administration machinery had been introduced by the Great Revolution and had been wielded especially by the Convention as an indispensable and decisive weapon in defeating the royalist and federative reaction and the external foe. But to-day it is a well-known fact that during the entire revolution until the eighteenth of Brumaire the whole of administration of the departments, arrondissements and municipalities consisted of bodies which had been elected by those administered, which moved with perfect freedom within the general state laws; that this provincial and local self-government, which was similar to that in America, became precisely the strongest of all levers of the revolution, to such an extent that Napoleon immediately after his coup d'état of the eighteenth of Brumaire hastened to replace it by the still existing system of prefects, which therefore was a pure instrument of reaction from its very inception. But local and provincial home-rule no more contradicts political, national centralization than it is necessarily connected with that narrow-minded cantonal and municipal self-seeking which we encounter with so much disgust in Switzerland and which in 1849 all South-German federative republicans in Germany wanted to make the rule. (Note by Engels to the Zurich edition of 1885. – *Ed.*)

measures. But they can:

1. Force the democrats to interfere in as many directions as possible in the heretofore existing order of society, to impede its regular course and to compromise themselves and to concentrate in the hands of the state the greatest number of productive forces, means of transport, factories, railways, etc.

2. They must bring to a head the proposals of the democrats who in any event will not act in a revolutionary but only reformist manner and must convert them into direct attacks against private property; for instance when the petty bourgeoisie proposes to buy up the railways and factories, the workers must demand that these railways and factories be simply confiscated by the state without compensation as the property of reactionaries. If the democrats propose proportional taxation the workers must demand progressive taxation; if the democrats themselves come out in favor of moderate progressive taxation, the workers must insist on a tax, the gradations of which will rise so rapidly that big capital will be ruined by it; if the democrats will demand the settlement of the government debt, the workers must demand the bankruptcy of the state. The demands of the workers must therefore be guided everywhere by the concessions and measures of the democrats.

If the German workers cannot come to power and carry through their class interests without going wholly through a lengthy revolutionary development they at least have the assurance this time that the first act of this impending revolutionary spectacle coincides with the direct victory of their own class in France and is thereby greatly accelerated.

But they themselves must contribute most to their ultimate victory by seeking enlightenment about their class interests, by occupying their independent party position as soon as possible, by not allowing themselves to be misled for a moment by the hypocritical phrases of the democratic petty bourgeoisie in their pursuit of the independent organization of the party of the proletariat. Their battle cry must be: The Revolution in Permanence.

London, March, 1850.

Karl Marx, *Revelations Concerning the Communist Trial at Cologne* (Appendix).

C. Struggle of the Proletariat for the Revolutionary-Democratic Dictatorship of the Proletariat and Peasantry – The Fight for the Growing of the Bourgeois-Democratic Revolution Into the Socialist Revolution

Marxism teaches the proletarian not to keep aloof from the bourgeois revolution, not to refuse to take part in it, not to allow the leadership of the revolution to be assumed by the bourgeoisie, but, on the contrary, to take a most energetic part in it, to fight resolutely for consistent proletarian democracy, to fight to carry the revolution to its completion. We cannot jump out of the bourgeois-democratic boundaries of the Russian revolution, but we can enormously extend those boundaries and within these boundaries we can and must fight for the interests of the proletariat, for its immediate needs and for the prerequisites for training its forces for the complete victory that is to come. There are different kinds of bourgeois democracy. The Monarchist Zemstvo member,[*] who advocated an Upper Chamber, who is "haggling" for universal suffrage and who in secret, *sub rosa,* is striking a bargain with tsarism for a restricted Constitution, is a bourgeois democrat. And the peasant who is carrying on an armed struggle against the landlords and the government officials and in a "naive republican fashion" proposes to "kick out the tsar" is also a bourgeois democrat. The bourgeois-democratic regime varies in different countries – in Germany and in England, in Austria and in America or Switzerland. He would be a fine Marxist indeed, who in a democratic revolution failed to see the difference between the degrees of democracy, between the different nature of this or that form of it, and confined himself to "clever" quips about this after all being "a bourgeois revolution," the fruits of a "bourgeois revolution."

Our new *Iskra*-ists are precisely such wiseacres, proud of their short-sightedness. It is they who confine themselves to disquisitions on the bourgeois character of the revolution, on the questions as to when and where one must be able to draw a distinction between

---

[*] Zemstvo – rural local authorities, set up in the sixties after the emancipation of the serfs, and representing exclusively the landowning interests. They appeared at various periods as more or less active though moderate opponents of the autocracy. Most of the leaders of the bourgeois political parties which sprang up after October, 1905, emerged from and received their political training in the ranks of the Zemstvo. – *Ed.*

republican-revolutionary and monarchist-liberal bourgeois democracy, not to mention the distinction between inconsistent bourgeois democracy and consistent proletarian democracy. They are satisfied – as if they had really become like the "man in the box"[*] – to converse dolefully about the "process of mutual struggle of the conflicting classes," when what is needed is to give a *democratic lead* in a real revolution, to emphasize the *progressive democratic* slogans as distinguished from the treacherous slogans of Messrs. Struve and Co., to state straightforwardly and trenchantly the immediate tasks of the actual revolutionary struggle of the proletariat and the peasantry, as distinguished from the liberal brokers' tactics of the landlords and manufacturers. At the present time the crux of the matter lies in the following, which you, gentlemen, have missed, *viz.,* whether our revolution will result in a real, great victory, or in a miserable bargain, whether it will go as far as the revolutionary democratic dictatorship of the proletariat and the peasantry, or whether it will exhaust itself in a liberal constitution "a la Shipov."

What is a "decisive victory of the revolution over tsarism"? We have already seen that in using this expression the new *Iskra*-ists do not grasp even its immediate political significance. Still less do they seem to understand the class content of this concept. Surely we Marxists must not allow ourselves to be deluded by *words,* such as "revolution," or "the great Russian revolution," as many revolutionary democrats (of the type of Gapon[†]) do.

We must be perfectly clear in our own minds as to what real social forces are opposed to "tsarism" (which is a real force, perfectly intelligible to all) and are capable of gaining a "decisive victory" over it. Such a force cannot be the big bourgeoisie, the landlords, the manufacturers, not "society" which follows the lead of *Osvobozhdeniye-ists.* We see that these do not even want a decisive victory. We know that owing to their class position they are incapable of undertaking a decisive struggle against tsarism; they are too handicapped by the shackles of private property, capital and land to venture a decisive struggle. Tsarism with its bureaucratic police and

---

[*] Shut off from the world. The subject of one of Chekhov's short stories. – *Ed.*

[†] Priest, organizer of police-controlled unions and leader of the demonstration at the Winter Palace in St. Petersburg on January 22, 1905 ("Bloody Sunday"). – *Ed.*

military forces against the proletariat and the peasantry is far too necessary for them in their struggle for them to strive for the destruction of tsarism. No, only the *people* can constitute a force capable of gaining "a decisive victory over tsarism," in other words, the proletariat and the peasantry, if we take the main, big forces and distribute the rural and urban petty bourgeoisie (also falling under the category of "people") between both of the two forces. "The decisive victory of the revolution over tsarism" is *the revolutionary democratic dictatorship of the proletariat and peasantry.* Our new Iskra-ists will never be able to escape from this conclusion, which *Vperyod* pointed out long ago. There is no one else who is capable of gaining a decisive victory over tsarism.

And such victory will be precisely a dictatorship, *i.e.,* it is inevitably bound to rely on military force, on the arming of the masses, on an uprising, and not on institutions established by "lawful" or "peaceful" means. It can only be a dictatorship, for the introduction of the reforms which are urgently and absolutely necessary for the proletariat and the peasantry, will call forth the desperate resistance of the landlords, the big bourgeoisie and tsarism. Without a dictatorship it will be impossible to break down that resistance and to repel the counter-revolutionary attempts. But of course it will be a democratic, not a socialist dictatorship. It will not be able (without a series of intermediary stages of revolutionary development) to touch the foundation of capitalism. At best it may bring about a radical redistribution of the land to the advantage of the peasantry, establish consistent and full democracy including the republic, eliminate all the oppressive features of Asiatic bondage, not only of village but also of factory life, lay the foundation for thorough improvement in the position of the workers and raise their standard of living and, *last but not least** – carry the revolutionary conflagration into Europe. Such victory will by no means as yet transform our bourgeois revolution into a socialist revolution; the democratic revolution will not extend beyond the scope of bourgeois social and economic relations; nevertheless the significance of such a victory for the future development of Russia and of the whole world will be immense. Nothing will raise so much the revolutionary energy of the world proletariat, nothing will shorten so much the path leading to its complete victory, as this decisive victory of the revolution that has

---

* This phrase is given in English in the original text. – *Ed.*

now started in Russia.

Whether that victory is probable or not is another question. We are not the least inclined to be unreasonably optimistic on that score, we do not for a moment forget the immense difficulties of this task but since we are out to fight we must wish to win and must be able to indicate the proper path to victory. Tendencies capable of leading to such a victory undoubtedly exist. It is true that our social-democratic influence on the masses of the proletariat is as yet exceedingly inadequate; the revolutionary influence on the masses of the peasantry is altogether insignificant; the dispersion, backwardness and ignorance of the proletariat, and especially of the peasantry, are still enormous. But revolution consolidates and educates rapidly. Every step in the development of the revolution rouses the masses and attracts them with uncontrollable force precisely to the side of the revolutionary program as the only program that consistently and logically expresses their real, vital interests.

V. I. Lenin, *Two Tactics of Social Democracy in the Democratic Revolution,* Little Lenin Library, Vol. 22, Chap. VI, pp. 41-46.

D. Motive Force of the Bourgeois-Democratic and Motive Force of the Proletarian Revolution

The Russian revolution will be a bourgeois revolution, said all the Marxists in Russia before 1905. The Mensheviks, however, substituting Liberalism for Marxism, reasoned therefrom that consequently the proletariat must not go beyond what was acceptable to the bourgeoisie, and must pursue a policy of compromise with it. The Bolsheviks, on the other hand, argued that that was a bourgeois Liberal theory. The bourgeoisie, they said, was trying to effect a change of the State on bourgeois, on *reformist,* not on revolutionary lines, by preserving, so far as possible, the monarchy, landlordism, etc. The proletariat must not allow itself to be hamstrung by the reformism of the bourgeoisie but must carry through the bourgeois-democratic revolution to the end. As for the *class* correlation of forces in the time of bourgeois revolution, the Bolsheviks gave the following formula: The proletariat, by gaining the adhesion of the peasantry, would neutralize the Liberal bourgeoisie, and would raze to the ground the monarchy, landlordism, and all the survivals of the Middle Ages.

The *bourgeois* character of the revolution will be manifested precisely in this alliance of the proletariat with the peasantry *as a whole,* since the peasantry as a whole consists of small producers who adhere to the system of commodity production. Subsequently, the Bolsheviks were arguing further, the proletariat would ally with itself the entire semi-*proletariat* (that is, all those who are exploited and toil), would neutralize the middle peasantry and would *overthrow* the bourgeoisie: this would be the Socialist revolution, as distinguished from the bourgeois democratic revolution (see my pamphlet: *Two Tactics,* issued in 1905, and reprinted at Petrograd in 1907, in the collected volume: *Twelve Years*).

V. I. Lenin, *The Proletarian Revolution and Renegade Kautsky,* Little Lenin Library, Vol. 21, pp. 73-74.

E. Lenin on the Growing of the Bourgeois-Democratic Revolution into the Socialist Revolution in 1905

...We support the peasant movement, in so far as it is revolutionary and democratic. We are making ready (making ready at once, immediately) to fight against it in so far as it becomes reactionary and anti-proletarian. The whole essence of Marxism lies in that two-fold task, which only those who do not understand Marxism can vulgarize or compress into one simple task.

Let us take a concrete instance. Let us assume that the peasant uprising is victorious. The revolutionary peasant committees and the provisional revolutionary government (partly leaning on these very committees) is able to carry out the confiscation of all big property. We stand for confiscation, we have declared so already. But to whom shall we recommend that the confiscated land be given? We have not tied our hands on this question and never shall do so by declarations like those uncautiously proposed by the author of the letter. The author has forgotten that the same resolution of the Third Congress speaks firstly of *"purging the revolutionary democratic content of the peasant movement of all reactionary admixtures,"* and, secondly, of the necessity *"in all cases and under all circumstances for an independent organization of the rural proletariat."* Such are our directives. There will always be reactionary admixtures in the peasant movement, and we declare war on them in advance. Class antagonism between the rural proletariat and the peasant bourgeoisie is inevitable, and we reveal it in advance, explain it *and make ready for the struggle on the basis of this antagonism.*

One of the causes of such struggle may very likely be the question: to whom the confiscated land is to be given and how? We do not gloss over that question, we do not promise equal distribution, "socialization," etc. What we say is this: we shall fight later on, we shall fight again, on a new field, and with other allies. Then we shall certainly be with the rural proletariat, with the whole of the working class *against* the peasant bourgeoisie. Practically, this may mean the transfer of the land to the class of petty peasant proprietors – wherever the big estates based on bondage and servitude still predominate, where there are as yet no material prerequisites for large scale Socialist production; it may mean nationalization – provided there is a complete victory of the democratic revolution; or the big capitalist estates may be transferred to *workers' associations,* for from the democratic revolution we shall at once, – according to the degree of our strength, the strength of the class conscious organized proletariat, – begin to pass to the socialist revolution. We stand for continuous revolution. We shall not stop halfway. The reason we do not promise now, immediately, all sorts of "socialization," is precisely that we do know the real conditions that are required for that task and that we do not gloss over but reveal the new class struggle that is maturing within the womb of the peasantry.

At first we support to the end by all means, including confiscation, the peasantry generally against the landlords and then (or even not "then," but at the same time) we support the proletariat against the peasantry in general. To try *now* to calculate the combination of forces among the peasantry on "the morrow" of the (democratic) revolution is sheer Utopia. Without indulging in any adventures or being false to our scientific conscience, without striving after cheap popularity, we can and do say *only one thing:* we will with all our might help the entire peasantry to make the democratic revolution *in order that it may be easier* for us, the party of the proletariat, to pass on, as soon as possible, to a new and higher task – the socialist revolution. We do not promise harmony, equality, "socialization" as a result of the victory of the *present* peasant uprising, – on the contrary, we "promise" a new struggle, new inequality, a new revolution, towards which we are striving. Our doctrine is not "sweet" as the tales of the Socialist-Revolutionaries, but whoever wants to be fed entirely on sweets, let him join the Socialist-Revolutionaries: we shall say to such people, – good riddance.

V. I. Lenin, "The Attitude of Social Democracy Towards the Peasant Movement," *Selected Works,* Vol. III.

3. Struggle of the Party Against Distortions of the Leninist Theory and Tactic of the Growing of the Bourgeois-Democratic Revolution into the Proletarian Revolution

A. Struggle against the Trotskyist Theory of the Permanent Revolution

In the book *Foundations of Leninism,* the "theory of permanent revolution" is appraised as one which underestimates the role of the peasantry. There it is stated:

> Lenin, then, fought the adherents of "permanent" revolution not over the question of "uninterruptedness," because he himself held the point of view of uninterrupted revolution, but because they underestimated the role of the peasantry, the proletariat's greatest reserve power....

This characterization of the Russian "permanentists" was considered as generally accepted until recently. Nevertheless, though generally correct, it cannot be regarded as exhaustive. On the one hand, the discussion of 1924, and, on the other hand, a detailed analysis of the works of Lenin, have shown that the mistake of the Russian "permanentists" consisted not only in their underestimation of the role of the peasantry, but also in their underestimation of the strength and ability of the proletariat to lead the peasantry, and their lack of faith in the idea of the hegemony of the proletariat.

For this reason, in my pamphlet, the *October Revolution and the Tactics of the Russian Communists* (1924), I broadened this characterization, replacing by another, more exhaustive one.

This is what is said on this point in the pamphlet:

> Hitherto only *one* side of the theory of "permanent revolution" has commonly been noted – lack of faith in the revolutionary possibilities inherent in the peasant movement. Now, in fairness this side must be supplemented by *another* side – lack of faith in the strength and capacities of the proletariat in Russia. (Stalin, *The October Revolution,* p. 111.)

Of course, this does not mean that Leninism has been or is opposed to the idea of permanent revolution, without quotation marks, as proclaimed by Marx in the forties of the last century. On the contrary, Lenin was the only Marxist who correctly understood and developed the idea of permanent revolution. What distinguishes Lenin from the "permanentists" on this question is that these latter distorted Marx's idea of permanent revolution and transformed it into lifeless, bookish wisdom, whereas Lenin took it in its pure form and made it one of the bases of his own theory of revolution. It should be remembered that the idea of the bourgeois-democratic revolution growing into the socialist revolution, propounded by Lenin as long ago as 1905, is one of the forms of the embodiment of the Marxist theory of permanent revolution. Here is what Lenin wrote about this in 1905:

> ...from the democratic revolution we shall at once, – according to the degree of our strength, the strength of the class conscious organized proletariat, – begin to pass to the socialist revolution. *We stand for continuous revolution* [Emphasis mine. – *J. S.*]. We shall not stop halfway.... Without indulging in any adventures or being false to our scientific conscience, without striving after cheap popularity, we can and do say *only one thing:* we will with all our might help the entire peasantry to make the democratic revolution *in order that it may be easier* for us, the party of the proletariat, to pass on, as soon as possible, to a new and higher task – the socialist revolution. ("The Attitude of Social-Democracy Towards the Peasant Movement," *Selected Works,* Vol. III.)

Writing on the same topic sixteen years later, after the conquest of power by the proletariat, Lenin stated:

> The Kautskys, Hilferdings, Martovs, Chernovs, Hillquits, Longuets, MacDonalds, Turatis, and other heroes of "Two-and-a-Half" Marxism have failed to understand the relationship between the bourgeois-democratic revolution and the proletarian-socialist revolution. *The first grows into the second* [Emphasis mine. – *J. S.*]. The second, in passing, solves the problem of the first. The second consolidates the work of the first. Struggle, and nothing but struggle, decides how far the second succeeds in outgrowing the first. (*Collected Works,* Russian edition, Vol. XXVII, p. 26.)

I wish to draw special attention to the first of the foregoing quotations, which is taken from an article by Lenin entitled, *The Attitude of Social-Democracy Towards the Peasant Movement,* published on September 1, 1905. I emphasize this for the information of those comrades who still continue to assert that Lenin only arrived at the idea of the bourgeois-democratic revolution growing into the socialist revolution, the idea of permanent revolution, after the outbreak of the imperialist war, somewhere about the year 1916. The quotation leaves no doubt that these comrades are profoundly mistaken.

Joseph Stalin, *Problems of Leninism,* Chap. III.

B. Lenin's Fight in 1917 Against the Rights' Repudiation of the Strategic Plan Concerning the Growing of the Bourgeois-Democratic Revolution into the Proletarian Revolution

Let us now see how Comrade U. Kamenev formulates his "disagreements" with my theses and with the above-expressed views in his short article in No. 27 of the *Pravda.* This will help us to clarify them with more exactness.

"As regards Comrade Lenin's general scheme," writes Comrade Kamenev, "it appears to us unacceptable, inasmuch as it proceeds from the assumption that the bourgeois-democratic revolution *has been completed,* and it builds on the immediate transformation of this revolution into a Socialist revolution."

There are two major errors in this.

1. The question of a "completed," bourgeois-democratic revolution is stated wrongly. The question is put in an abstract, simple, if we may say so, monochromatic way, which does not correspond to the objective reality. Any one who puts the question in this way, who *now* asks whether the bourgeois-democratic revolution has been completed, *and nothing further,* deprives himself of the possibility of understanding the extraordinarily complicated actuality which has at least two colors. This – in theory. In practice, he capitulates helplessly to *petty-bourgeois revolutionism.*

As a matter of fact, reality shows us *both* the passing of the power into the hands of the bourgeoisie (a "completed" bourgeois-democratic revolution of the ordinary type) *and,* by the side of the actual government, the existence of a parallel government which represents the "revolutionary-democratic dictatorship of the proletariat and the peasantry." This latter "also government" has *itself* ceded power to the bourgeoisie, itself voluntarily chained itself to the bourgeois government.

Is this reality embraced in the old Bolshevik formula of Comrade Kamenev that "the bourgeois-democratic revolution is not completed"?

No, the formula is antiquated. It is good for nothing. It is dead. Attempts to revive it will be in vain.

2. A practical question. It is not known whether it is possible at present for a *special* "revolutionary-democratic dictatorship of the proletariat and the peasantry," detached from the bourgeois government, to exist in Russia? Marxian tactics must not be based on the unknown.

But *if* this is still possible, then there is one, and only one way toward it, namely, a direct, resolute, irrevocable separation of the proletarian Communist elements of the movement from the petty-bourgeois elements.

Why?

Because the whole petty bourgeoisie has, not by chance but of necessity, turned toward chauvinism (defencism), towards "supporting" the bourgeoisie, towards depending on it, towards the *fear* of not getting on without it, etc.

How can the petty bourgeoisie be "pushed" into power, when this petty bourgeoisie can seize power *now,* but does not want to?

Only by separating the proletarian Communist Party, through proletarian class struggle *free* from the timidity of those petty-bourgeois, only by consolidating the proletarians who are free from the influence of the petty bourgeoisie in deed and not only in word – can one make things so "hot" for the petty bourgeoisie that, in certain circumstances, it will *have to* seize power; it is not even out of the question that Guchkov and Milyukov – again in certain circumstances – should stand for all power, for sole power being given to Chkheidze, Tsereteli, the Socialist-Revolutionaries, Steklov, because after all they are all *"defencists"!*

Any one who, right now, immediately and irrevocably, separates the proletarian elements of the Soviets (*i.e.,* the proletarian Communist Party) from the petty-bourgeois elements, provides a correct expression of the interests of the movement for both possible cases: for the case when Russia still goes through a special "dictatorship of the proletariat and the peasantry" independent of and not subordinate to the bourgeoisie, and for the case when the petty bourgeoisie is not able to detach itself from the bourgeoisie and swings eternally (that is, until socialism) between us and it.

Any one who is guided in his activities by the simple formula, "the bourgeois-democratic revolution is not completed," vouches, as it were, that the petty bourgeoisie will certainly be capable of being independent of the bourgeoisie. In doing so, he at once surrenders to the mercy of the petty bourgeoisie.

Apropos: With regard to the "formula" of the dictatorship of the proletariat and the peasantry, it would not be amiss to recall that, in my article "Two Tactics" (July, 1905) I specially emphasized:

> The revolutionary-democratic dictatorship of the proletariat and the peasantry has, like everything else in the world, a past and a future. Its past is absolutism, feudalism, monarchy, privileges.... Its future – the struggle against private property, the struggle of the wage-earners against the employers, the struggle for Socialism....

The mistake made by Comrade Kamenev is that in 1917 he only sees the *past* of the revolutionary-democratic dictatorship of the proletariat and the peasantry. In reality, however, its *future* has already begun, for the interests and the policy of the wage-earners and the petty proprietors have actually already taken different lines, and that in such an important question as "defencism," the attitude towards the imperialist war.

This brings me to the second mistake in the remarks of Comrade Kamenev quoted above: He reproaches me, saying that my scheme "builds" on "the immediate transformation of this (bourgeois-democratic) revolution into a Socialist revolution."

This is not true. Not only do I not "build" on the "immediate transformation" of our revolution into a *Socialist* one, but I directly caution against it, when in Thesis No. 8, I directly state: *"Not* the 'introduction' of Socialism as our immediate task...."

Is it not clear that any one who builds on the immediate transformation of our revolution into a Socialist one could not oppose the immediate task of introducing Socialism?

An idle question put in a false way. I "build" *only* on this, *exclusively* on this – that the workers, soldiers and peasants will deal better than the officials, better than the police, with the practical, difficult problems of increasing the production of foodstuffs, their better distribution, the more satisfactory provisioning of the soldiers, etc., etc.

I am deeply convinced that the Soviets of Workers, etc., Deputies will make the independent activity of the masses a reality more quickly and effectively than will a parliamentary republic (I will compare the two types of state in greater detail in another letter). They will more effectively, more practically and more correctly decide what *steps* can be taken toward Socialism and how these steps should be taken. Control over a bank, amalgamation of all banks into one, is *not yet* Socialism, but it is a *step toward* Socialism. To-day such steps are being taken in Germany by the Junkers and the bourgeoisie against the people. To-morrow the Soviet of Workers' and Soldiers' Deputies will be able to take these steps much more effectively to the advantage of the people when the whole state power will be in its hands.

What *compels* the taking of such steps?

Famine. Economic disorganization. Threatening collapse. War horrors. Horrors of the wounds inflicted on mankind by the war.

Comrade Kamenev concludes his article with the remark that "in a broad discussion he hopes to carry his point of view as the only possible one for revolutionary Social-Democracy in so far as it wishes to be and must remain to the very end the party of the revolutionary masses of the proletariat without turning into a group of Communist propagandists."

It seems to me that these words betray a completely erroneous estimate of the situation. Comrade Kamenev contrasts a "party of the masses" with a "group of propagandists." Still, just now the "masses" have yielded to the frenzy of "revolutionary" defencism. Is it not more worthy of internationalists at this moment to be able to resist "mass" frenzy rather than to "wish to remain" with the masses, *i.e.,* to yield to the general epidemic? Have we not witnessed how in all the belligerent countries of Europe the chauvinists justified themselves by their wish to "remain with the masses"? Is it not our duty to be able to remain for a while in the minority against a "mass" frenzy? Is it not the work of precisely the propagandists just at the present moment the central issue for clearing the proletarian line from the defencist and petty-bourgeois "mass" frenzy? It was just this fusion of the masses, proletarian and non-proletarian, without distinction of class differences inside of the masses, that formed one of the conditions for the defencist epidemic. To speak with contempt of a "group of propagandists" of the *proletarian* line does not seem to be very becoming.

V. I. Lenin, "Letters on Tactics," *Collected Works,* Vol. XX, Book I, pp. 125-129.

C. Lenin's Struggle Against the Strikebreaking Position of Kamenev and Zinoviev in 1917

Comrades! Yesterday, November 17 (4), several members of the C.C. of our Party and of the Council of People's Commissars – Kamenev, Zinoviev, Nogin, Rykov, Miliutin and a few others – withdrew from the C.C. of our Party and the three last-named from the Council of People's Commissars.

In so great a Party as ours, despite the proletarian-revolutionary course of our policy, individual comrades insufficiently staunch and stern in the struggle against the enemies of the people were bound to crop up. The tasks which at present confront our Party are truly immeasurable, the difficulties are immense – and some of the members of our Party who formerly occupied responsible posts have flinched before the onslaught of the bourgeoisie and fled from our midst. All the bourgeoisie and all its servitors rejoice at this, laugh with malicious glee, shout collapse, prophesy the downfall of the Bolshevik government.

Comrades! Do not believe this lie. The comrades who have left have acted like deserters, not only having abandoned the posts entrusted to them, but also having acted contrary to the direct decision of the C.C. of our Party to defer the withdrawal at least until the decision of the Petrograd and Moscow Party organizations. We emphatically condemn this desertion. We are profoundly convinced that all class-conscious workers, soldiers and peasants who belong to our Party or who are in sympathy with it will likewise emphatically condemn the conduct of the deserters.

But we declare that the deserters' conduct of several members of the leading circles of our Party will not for a moment nor for a hair's-breadth shake the unity of the *masses* which follow our Party, and consequently will not shake our Party.

Bear in mind, Comrades, that two of the deserters, Kamenev and Zinoviev, already before the uprising in Petrograd came out like deserters and strike-breakers, for they not only voted against the uprising, at the decisive meeting of the C.C. on October 23 (10), 1917, but also *after* the decision of the C.C. had been taken, they agitated before Party workers against the uprising. Everybody knows that newspapers which were afraid to take the side of the workers and which inclined more to the side of the bourgeoisie (as for instance the *Novaya Zhizn*) at that time raised a hullabaloo together with the entire bourgeois press about the "collapse of the uprising," etc. But life quickly refuted the lies and slander of some, and the doubts, vacillations and cowardice of others. The "storm" which they wanted to raise anent the steps taken by Kamenev and Zinoviev towards the undermining of the Petrograd uprising proved to be a *storm in a teacup,* and the great upsurge of the masses, the great heroism of the millions of workers, soldiers and peasants in St. Petersburg and Moscow, at the front, in the trenches and in the villages, brushed aside the deserters with the ease with which a railway train sweeps aside chips of wood.

Let them be ashamed – all those of little faith, all those who vacillate, all those who doubt, all those who permitted the bourgeoisie to frighten them or those who succumbed to the cries of its direct and indirect servitors. *There is not* an iota of wavering among the *masses* of Petrograd, Moscow or other workers and soldiers. Our Party to a man, firm and united, stands guard over the Soviet government, over the interests of all the toilers, primarily the workers and the poorest peasants.

V. I. Lenin, "From the Central Committee of the Russian Social-Democratic Labor Party [Bolsheviks]," 1917, *Collected Works,* Vol. XXII, Russian edition.

D. The Struggle of the Party Against the Trotskyist Slander
Concerning the Re-equipment of the Bolsheviks in 1917

Thus we have the "re-equipment" of the Bolsheviks "beginning in 1917," on the basis of the theory of the permanent revolution; the delivery of the Bolsheviks, in connection with this, from the "anti-revolutionary features of Bolshevism"; and finally, the "confirmation" in its entirety of the theory of the permanent revolution" – such is Trotsky's conclusion.

But where did Leninism, the theory of Bolshevism, the Bolshevik appraisal of our revolution, of its moving forces, etc., get to? They either "were not confirmed in their entirety," or were not "confirmed" at all, or were scattered into thin air, yielding their place on the subject of the "re-equipment" of the Party to the theory of permanent revolution.

And thus, once upon a time, there were Bolsheviks; they somehow or other, "beginning" in 1903, "hammered together" a party; but they had no revolutionary theory; so "beginning" in 1903 they kept on and somehow they managed to get to the year 1917; then, when they noticed Comrade Trotsky holding the theory of the permanent revolution in his hands, they decided to "re-equip" themselves and in "re-equipping" themselves lost the last remnants of Leninism, of the Leninist theory of revolution and thus brought about the "complete coincidence" of the theory of permanent revolution and the "position" of our Party.

This is a very interesting fairy tale, comrades. This, if you will, is one of the wonderful sleights of hand that can be observed in a circus. But, you see, we are not holding a circus but a conference of our Party. And we did not engage Comrade Trotsky as a circus performer. Why then these sleights of hand?

How did Comrade Lenin evaluate Trotsky's theory of permanent revolution? Here is what he writes in one of his articles about this theory, ridiculing it as an "original" and "excellent" theory:

"To make clear the interrelation of classes in the coming impending revolution is the main task of a revolutionary party. This task is incorrectly solved in the *Nashe Slovo* by Trotsky, who repeats his 'original' 1905 theory without stopping to think why life, during a whole decade, has gone past this beautiful theory.

"Trotsky's original theory takes from the Bolsheviks their appeal to decisive revolutionary struggle of the proletariat and to the conquest of political power by it; from the Mensheviks it takes the 'negation' of the role of the peasantry. Thereby, in practice, Trotsky aids the liberal labor politicians in Russia who by the 'negation' of the role of the peasantry understand a refusal to arouse the peasants to a revolution!" (Lenin, *Collected Works,* Vol. XVIII, pp. 362-63.)

It follows that, according to Lenin, the theory of permanent revolution is a semi-Menshevik theory which ignores the revolutionary role of the peasantry in the Russian revolution.

The only thing not intelligible is how this semi-Menshevik theory could "fully and completely coincide" with the position of our Party, at least "beginning with 1917."...

The only thing not intelligible is how such a theory could "re-equip" our Bolshevik Party.

Joseph Stalin, "On the Social-Democratic Deviation in Our Party," *On the Opposition.*

E. Stalin's Criticism of the Opportunist Position of Preobrazhensky in 1917

Comrade Stalin (reads clause 9 of the resolution):

"(9) The task of these revolutionary classes is then to devote all their forces to taking political power into their hands and to directing it, in union with the revolutionary proletariat of the advanced countries, towards peace and the socialist reconstruction of society."

Comrade Preobrazhensky: I propose a different wording for the last part of the resolution: "To direct it towards peace, and, provided there is a proletarian revolution in the West, towards socialism." If we adopt the wording of the Committee, then there will be disagreement with the resolution of Comrade Bukharin, which has already been adopted.

Comrade Stalin: I am against such a conclusion of the resolution. The possibility is not excluded that Russia may be the very country which will pave the way to socialism. Up to now no country has enjoyed such absolute freedom as there is in Russia, no country has tried to adopt workers' control of industry. Besides that, the basis of our revolution is broader than in Western Europe, where the proletariat stands face to face with the bourgeoisie in complete isolation. In our country the workers are supported by the poorest sections of the peasantry. Finally, in Germany the apparatus of state power works incomparably better than the imperfect apparatus of our bourgeoisie, which itself is tributary to European capital. We must reject the outworn conception that only Europe can show us the way. There is dogmatic Marxism and creative Marxism; I am on the side of the latter.

Chairman: I put the amendment of Comrade Preobrazhensky to a vote. Rejected.

The Eve of October, Sixth Congress of the Bolshevik Party, August, 1917, p. 47.

F. Exposing Trotskyist Contraband in the Theory of the Bourgeois-Democratic Revolution Growing into the Socialist Revolution

Trotskyism is the vanguard of the counter-revolutionary bourgeoisie.

That is why liberalism towards Trotskyism, even when the latter is shattered and concealed, is stupidly bordering on crime, bordering on treason to the working class.

That is why the attempts of certain "litterateurs" and "historians" to smuggle the disguised Trotskyist rubbish into our literature must encounter determined resistance from the Bolsheviks.

That is why we cannot admit a literary discussion with these Trotskyist smugglers.

It seems to me that "historians" and "litterateurs" of the category of the Trotskyist smugglers are for the present trying to carry on their work of smuggling along two lines.

First of all, they are trying to prove that Lenin in the period before the war underestimated the danger of centrism, while leaving the inexperienced reader to surmise that Lenin was not at that time a real revolutionary but became one only after the war, after he had been "re-equipped" with Trotsky's help. Slutski may be regarded as a typical representative of such a type of smuggler. We have seen above that Slutski and Co. are not worth our bothering about much.

Secondly, they try to prove that Lenin in the pre-war period did not understand the necessity for the bourgeois democratic revolution growing into the socialist revolution, while leaving the inexperienced reader to surmise that Lenin was not at that time a real Bolshevik, that he grasped the necessity for such a development only after the war, after he had been "re-equipped" with Trotsky's help. We may regard Volosevich, author of *Course of History of the C.P.S.U.,* as a typical representative of this sort of smuggler. It is true, Lenin as early as 1905 wrote that *"from the democratic revolution we shall at once, – according to the degree of our strength, the strength of the class conscious organized 'proletariat, begin to pass to the socialist revolution,"* that *"we stand for continuous revolution, we shall not stop halfway."* It is true, a very great number of facts and documents of an analogous sort could be found in the works of Lenin, but what concern have people like Volosevich for the facts from the life and activity of Lenin? People like Volosevich write in order, by camouflaging themselves in Bolshevik colors, to drag in their anti-Leninist contraband, to lie against the Bolsheviks and falsify the history of the Bolshevik Party.

Joseph Stalin, "Questions Concerning the History of Bolshevism," *Leninism,* Vol. II.

IV. THE REVOLUTIONARY CRISIS AND ITS MATURING AT THE PRESENT STAGE

1. Lenin on a Revolutionary Situation

For a Marxist there is no doubt that a revolution is impossible without a revolutionary situation; furthermore, not every revolutionary situation leads to revolution. What are, generally speaking, the characteristics of a revolutionary situation? We can hardly be mistaken when we indicate the following three outstanding signs: (1) it is impossible for the ruling classes to maintain their power unchanged; there is a crisis of the "upper classes" taking one form or another; there is a crisis in the policy of the ruling class; as a result, there appears a crack through which the dissatisfaction and the indignation of the oppressed classes burst forth. If a revolution is to take place, it is usually insufficient that "the lower classes do not wish," but it is necessary that "the upper classes be unable" to continue in the old way; (2) the wants and sufferings of the oppressed classes become more acute than usual; (3) in consequence of the above causes, there is a considerable increase in the activity of the masses who in "peace time" allow themselves to be robbed without protest, but in stormy times are drawn both by the conditions of the crisis and *by the "upper classes" themselves* into independent historic action.

Without these objective changes, which are independent not only of the will of separate groups and parties but even of separate classes, a revolution, as a rule, is impossible. The coexistence of all these objective changes is called a revolutionary situation. This situation existed in 1905 in Russia and in all the periods of revolution in the West, but it also existed in the sixties of the last century in Germany; it existed in 1859-61 and in 1879-80 in Russia, though there was no revolution in these latter instances. Why? Because a revolution emerges not out of every revolutionary situation, but out of such situations where, to the objective changes mentioned above, subjective ones are added, namely, the ability of the revolutionary *class* to carry out revolutionary mass actions *strong* enough to break (or to crack) the old government, which never, not even in a period of crises, "falls" unless it is "dropped."

V. I. Lenin, "Collapse of the Second International," *Collected Works,* Vol. XVIII.

The fundamental law of revolution, confirmed by all revolutions and particularly by all three Russian revolutions in the twentieth century, is as follows: it is not sufficient for revolution that the exploited and oppressed masses understand the impossibility of living in the old way and demand changes; for revolution, it is necessary that the exploiters should not be able to live and rule in the old way. Only when the "lower classes" *do not want* the old and when the "upper classes" cannot *continue in the old way,* then only can revolution succeed. This truth may be expressed in other words: revolution is impossible without a national crisis affecting both the exploited and the exploiters. It follows that for revolution it is essential, first, that a majority of the workers (or at least a majority of the class conscious, thinking, politically active workers) should fully understand the necessity for revolution and be ready to sacrifice their lives for it; secondly, that the ruling classes be in a state of government crisis which draws even the most backward masses into politics (a symptom of every real revolution is: the rapid tenfold and even hundredfold increase in the number of hitherto apathetic representatives of the toiling and oppressed masses capable of waging the political struggle), weakens the government and makes it possible for the revolutionaries to overthrow it rapidly.

...If it is a question of the practical activities of the masses, a question of the disposition, if one may so express it, of vast armies, of the alignment of *all* the class forces of the given society *for the final and decisive battle,* then propaganda alone, the mere repetition of the truths of "pure" communism are of no avail. In these circumstances one must count, not up to a thousand – as is really done by the propagandist who belongs to a small group which does not yet lead the masses; but one must count in millions and tens of millions. In these circumstances one must not only ask oneself whether the vanguard of the revolutionary class has been convinced, but also whether the historically effective forces of *all* classes – positively of all the classes in the given society without exception – are aligned in such a way that the decisive battle is fully matured, in such a way that (1) all the class forces hostile to us have become sufficiently confused, are sufficiently at loggerheads with each other, have sufficiently weakened themselves in a struggle beyond their capacities; that (2) all the vacillating, wavering, unstable, intermediate elements – the petty bourgeoisie and the petty-bourgeois democracy as distinct from the bourgeoisie – have sufficiently exposed themselves before the people and have sufficiently disgraced themselves through their practical bankruptcy; and that (3) among the proletariat a mass mood in favor of supporting the most determined, unreservedly bold, revolutionary action against the bourgeoisie has arisen and begins to grow powerfully. Then, indeed, revolution is ripe; then, indeed, if we have correctly gauged all the conditions briefly outlined above and if we have chosen the moment rightly, our victory is assured.

...The main task of contemporary Communism in Western Europe and America is to acquire the ability to seek, to find, to determine correctly the concrete path, or the particular turn of events that will *bring* the masses *right up* to the real, decisive, last and great revolutionary struggle.

Take England, for example: We cannot say, and no one is in a position to say beforehand how soon the real proletarian revolution will flare up there and *what* will serve as the *cause* to rouse it, to kindle it and move into the struggle very wide masses who are at present dormant. Hence, it is our duty to carry on our preparatory work in such a manner as to be "well shod on all four legs," as the late Plekhanov was fond of saying when he was a Marxist and revolutionary. It is possible that a parliamentary crisis will cause the "breach," will "break the ice." Perhaps it will be a crisis caused by the hopelessly entangled and increasingly painful and acute colonial and imperialist contradiction; perhaps some third cause, etc. We are not discussing the kind of struggle that will *determine* the fate of the proletarian revolution in England (not a single Communist has any doubts on that score; as far as we are concerned, this question is settled and definitely settled). What we are discussing is the *immediate cause* that will rouse the at present dormant proletarian masses and bring them right up to the revolution.

Let us not forget that in the bourgeois French Republic for example, in a situation which, from both the international and national aspect was a hundred times less revolutionary than the present one, one out of the thousands and thousands of dishonest tricks the reactionary military caste play (the Dreyfus case) was enough to serve as the "unexpected" and "petty" cause which brought the people to the verge of civil war!*

---

* Editor's Note: The Right opportunists did not understand this Leninist, dialectical posing of the question, but, on the basis of their theory of

111

In England, also, it is necessary to organize in a new way, not in a socialist manner but in a communist manner, not in a reformist manner but in a revolutionary manner the work of propaganda, agitation and organization among the armed forces and among the oppressed and disfranchised nationalities in "one's own" state (Ireland, the colonies). Because in all these spheres of social life, in the epoch of imperialism generally, and particularly now, after the war which tortured nationalities and quickly opened their eyes to the truth (*viz.*, tens of millions killed and maimed only for the purpose of deciding whether the British or German pirates shall plunder the largest number of countries) – all these spheres of social life are particularly becoming filled with inflammable material and create numerous causes of conflict, crises and the intensification of the class struggle. We do not know and we cannot know which spark – out of the innumerable sparks that are flying around in all countries as a result of the political and economic world crises – will kindle the conflagration, in the sense of specially rousing the masses, and we must, therefore, with the aid of our new, communist principles, set to work to "stir up" all, even the oldest, mustiest and seemingly hopeless spheres, for otherwise we shall not be able to cope with our tasks, we will not be all-sided, we will not be able to master all weapons and we will not be prepared either for victory of the bourgeoisie (which arranged all sides of social life in a bourgeois way) nor for the forthcoming communist reorganization of the whole of social life after the victory.

V. I. Lenin, *Left-Wing Communism: An Infantile Disorder,* Little Lenin Library, Vol. 20, Chaps. IX and X.

---

organized capitalism, asserted that a revolution could arise only out of a new imperialist war.

"Lenin," said Bukharin, the theorist of Right opportunism, "was not a whit afraid of being suspected of opportunism or some similar mortal sin and wrote that the victorious imperialist states would 'be successful' while on the other hand he noted the contradictions which capitalist stabilization gave rise to. And – what is of interest – Lenin connected the following revolutionary outbreak directly with the on-coming war.

"As for great popular movements, he sought them in the first place in the East; there he saw a revolutionary situation and the possibility of direct eruptions of great masses of the population. Has not history fully confirmed this prognosis?" (Bukharin, *Political Testament,* Part III.)

112

No impassable line should be drawn between a "revolutionary upsurge" and a "directly revolutionary situation." It cannot be said: "Up to this point we have a revolutionary upsurge; beyond that – a leap into a directly revolutionary situation." Only scholastics can put the question that way. Usually the former passes "unnoticeably" on to the latter. The task consists in preparing the proletariat even now for the decisive revolutionary battles without waiting for the moment when the so-called direct revolutionary situation will "arrive."

Joseph Stalin, *Replies to the Questions of the Sverdlov Students*, 1930.

2. Lenin on the Armed Uprising as the Highest Plane of a Revolutionary Crisis

Among the most vicious and perhaps most widespread distortions of Marxism practiced by the prevailing "Socialist" parties, is to be found the opportunist lie which says that preparations for an uprising, and generally the treatment of an uprising as an art, is "Blanquism."[*]

Bernstein, the leader of opportunism, long since gained sad notoriety by accusing Marxism of Blanquism; and our present opportunists, by shouting about Blanquism, in substance do not by one iota refurbish or "enrich" the meager "ideas" of Bernstein.

To accuse Marxists of Blanquism for treating uprising as an art! Can there be a more flagrant distortion of the truth, when there is not a single Marxist who denies that it was precisely Marx who expressed himself in the most definite, exact and categorical manner on this score; that it was Marx who called uprising precisely an *art,* who said that uprising must be treated as an art, that one must *gain* the first success and then proceed from success to success without stopping the *offensive* against the enemy and making use of his confusion, etc., etc.?

To be successful, the uprising must be based not on a conspiracy, not on a party, but on the advanced class. This is the first point.

---

[*] The teachings of the French revolutionist, Auguste Blanqui (1805-1881), favoring the overthrow of the ruling power through secret plotting of revolutionaries rather than through preparation and organization of the masses led by a revolutionary party. – *Ed.*

The uprising must be based on the revolutionary upsurge of the people. This is the second point. The uprising must be based on the *crucial point* in the history of the maturing revolution, when the activity of the vanguard of the people is at its height, when the *vacillations* in the ranks of the enemies, and *in the ranks of the weak, half-hearted, undecided friends of the revolution are strongest.* This is the third point. It is in pointing out these three conditions as the way of approaching the question of an uprising, that Marxism differs from *Blanquism.*

But once these conditions exist, then to refuse to treat the uprising *as an art* means to betray Marxism and the revolution.

To show why precisely the period we are living in now must be recognized as the one when it is *obligatory* for the Party to recognize the *uprising* as placed on the order of the day by the course of objective events, and to treat uprising as an art – to show this, it will perhaps be best to use the method of comparison and to draw a parallel between July 16-17 and the September days.[*]

On July 16-17 it was possible, without trespassing against the truth, to put the question thus: it would have been more proper to take power, since our enemies would anyway accuse us of revolt and treat us as rebels. This, however, did not warrant a decision to take power at that time, because there were still lacking the objective conditions for a victorious uprising.

1. We did not yet have behind us the class that is the vanguard of the revolution.

We did not yet have a majority among the workers and soldiers of the capitals. Now we have a majority in both Soviets. It was created *only* by the history of July and August, by the experience of ruthless punishment meted out to the Bolsheviks, and by the experience of the Kornilov affairs.

2. At that time there was no general revolutionary upsurge of the people. Now there is, after the Kornilov affair. This is proven by the situation in the provinces and by the seizure of power by the Soviets in many localities.

3. At that time there were no *vacillations on* a serious, general, political scale among our enemies and among the half-hearted petty bourgeoisie. Now the vacillations are enormous; our main enemy,

---

[*] The strikes and demonstrations in July and the defeat of the Kornilov revolt in September. – *Ed.*

the imperialism of the Allies and of the world (for the "Allies" are at the head of world imperialism), has begun to *vacillate* between war to a victory and a separate peace against Russia. Our petty-bourgeois democrats, having obviously lost their majority among the people, have begun to vacillate enormously, rejecting a bloc, *i.e.,* a coalition with the Cadets.

4. This is why an uprising on July 16-17 would have been an error: we would not have retained power either physically or politically. Not physically, in spite of the fact that at certain moments Petrograd was in our hands, because our workers and soldiers would not have *fought and died* at that time for the sake of holding Petrograd; at that time people had not yet become so "brutalized"; there was not in existence such a burning hatred both towards the Kerenskys and towards the Tseretelis and Chernovs; and our own people were not yet hardened by the experience of the Bolsheviks being persecuted, while the Socialist-Revolutionaries and Mensheviks took part in the persecuting.

We could not have retained power July 16-17 politically, for, *before the Kornilov affairs,* the army and the provinces could and would have marched against Petrograd.

Now the picture is entirely different.

We have back of us the majority of a *class* that is the vanguard of the revolution, the vanguard of the people, and is capable of drawing the masses along.

We have back of us a *majority* of the people, for Chernov's exit, far from being the only sign, is only the most striking, the most outstanding sign showing that the peasantry *will not receive land* from a bloc with the S.-R.'s, or from the S.-R.'s themselves. And in this lies the essence of the popular character of the revolution.

We are in the advantageous position of a party which knows its road perfectly well; while *imperialism as a whole,* as well as the entire bloc of the Mensheviks and the S.-R.'s, is vacillating in an extraordinary manner.

Victory is assured to us, for the people are now very close to desperation, and we are showing the whole people a sure way out, having demonstrated to the whole people the significance of our leadership during the "Kornilov days," and then having *offered* the bloc politicians a compromise which they *rejected* at a time when their vacillations continued uninterruptedly.

It would be a very great error to think that our compromise offer has *not yet* been rejected, that the "Democratic Conference"[*] *still* may accept it. The compromise was offered from *party to parties.* It could not have been offered otherwise. The *parties* have rejected it. The Democratic Conference is nothing but a *conference.* One must not forget one thing, namely, that this conference does not represent the *majority* of the revolutionary people, the poorest and most embittered peasantry. One must not forget the self-evident truth that this conference represents a *minority of the people.* It would be a very great error, a very great parliamentary idiocy on our part, if we were to treat the Democratic Conference as a parliament, for even *if* it were to proclaim itself a parliament, the sovereign parliament of the revolution, it would not be able to *decide* anything. The decision lies *outside* of it, in the workers' sections of Petrograd and Moscow.

We have before us all the objective prerequisites for a successful uprising. We have the advantages of a situation where *only* our victory in an uprising will put an end to the most painful thing on earth, the vacillations that have sickened the people; a situation where *only our* victory in an uprising will *put an end* to the game of a separate peace against the revolution by openly offering a more complete, more just, more immediate peace *in favor* of the revolution.

Only our party, having won a victory in an uprising, *can* save Petrograd, for if our offer of peace is rejected, and we obtain not even a truce, then *we* shall become "defencists," then we shall place ourselves *at the head of the war parties,* we shall be the most "warring" party, and we shall carry on a war in a truly revolutionary manner. We shall take away from the capitalists all the bread and all the shoes. We shall leave them crumbs. We shall dress them in bast shoes. We shall send all the bread and all the shoes to the front.

And then we shall save Petrograd.

The resources, both material and spiritual, of a truly revolutionary war are still immense in Russia; there are ninety-nine chances in a hundred that the Germans will at least grant us a truce. And to secure a truce at present means to conquer the *whole world.*

Having recognized the absolute necessity of an uprising of the workers of Petrograd and Moscow for the sake of saving the revolution and of saving Russia from being "separately" divided among the imperialists of both coalitions, we must first adapt our political

---

[*] Called by the Kerensky government in the attempt to secure a broader base among the petty bourgeoisie following the Kornilov revolt. – *Ed.*

tactics at the conference to the conditions of the maturing uprising; secondly, we must prove that we accept, and not only in words, the idea of Marx about the necessity of treating uprising as an art.

At the conference, we must immediately consolidate the Bolshevik fraction without worrying about numbers, without being afraid of leaving the vacillators in the camp of the vacillating: they are more useful *there* to the cause of revolution than in the camp of the resolute and whole-hearted fighters.

We must compose a brief declaration in the name of the Bolsheviks in which we sharply emphasize the inopportuneness of long speeches, the inopportuneness of "speeches" generally, the necessity of quick action to save the revolution, the absolute necessity of breaking completely with the bourgeoisie, of completely ousting the whole present government, of completely severing relations with the Anglo-French imperialists who are preparing a "separate" partition of Russia, the necessity of all power immediately passing into the hands of *revolutionary democracy headed by the revolutionary proletariat.*

Our declaration must be the briefest and sharpest formulation of this conclusion; it must connect up with the points in the program of peace to the people, land to the peasants, confiscation of scandalous profits, and a halt to the scandalous damage to production done by the capitalists.

The briefer, the sharper the declaration, the better. Only two more important points must be clearly indicated in it, namely, that the people are tired of vacillations, that they are tortured by the lack of decisiveness on the part of the S.-R.'s and Mensheviks; and that we are definitely severing relations with these *parties* because they have betrayed the revolution.

The other point. In offering an immediate peace without annexations, in breaking at once with the Allied imperialists and with all imperialists, we obtain either an immediate truce or a going over of the entire revolutionary proletariat to the side of defense, and a truly just, truly revolutionary war will then be waged by revolutionary democracy under the leadership of the proletariat.

Having made this declaration, having appealed for *decisions* and not talk; for *actions,* not writing resolutions, we must *push* our whole fraction *into the factories and barracks:* its place is there; the pulse of life is there; the source of saving the revolution is there; the moving force of the Democratic Conference is there.

In heated, impassioned speeches we must make our program clear and we must put the question this way: either the conference accepts it *fully,* or an uprising follows. There is no middle course. Delay is impossible. The revolution is perishing.

Having put the question this way, having concentrated our entire fraction in the factories and barracks, *we shall correctly estimate the best moment to begin the uprising. .*

And in order to treat uprising in a Marxist way, *i.e.,* as an art, we must at the same time, without losing a single moment, organize the staff of the insurrectionary detachment; designate the forces; move the loyal regiments to the most important points; surround the Alexander Theater; occupy Peter and Paul Fortress; arrest the general staff and the government; move against the military cadets, the Wild Division, etc., such detachments as will die rather than allow the enemy to move to the center of the city; we must mobilize the armed workers, call them to a last desperate battle, occupy at once the telegraph and telephone stations, place *our* staff of the uprising at the central telephone station, connect it by wire with all the factories, the regiments, the points of armed fighting, etc.

Of course, this is all by way of an example, to *illustrate* the idea that at the present moment it is impossible to remain loyal to the revolution *without treating uprising as an art.*

V. I. Lenin, "Marxism and Uprising," *Collected Works,* Vol. XXI, Book I, pp. 224-229.

3. The Immediate Conditions of Victory of the Proletariat Shown by the Experience of the October Revolution of the Proletariat in Russia

COMRADES:

Our revolution is passing through a highly critical period. This crisis coincides with the great crisis – the maturing of the worldwide socialist revolution and the struggle waged against that revolution by world imperialism. A gigantic task is being imposed upon the responsible leaders of our Party, failure to perform which will involve the danger of a total collapse of the internationalist proletarian movement. The situation is such that, verily, procrastination is like unto death.

Take a glance at the international situation. The growth of a world revolution is beyond dispute. The outburst of indignation on the part of the Czech workers has been suppressed with incredible ferocity, which indicates the extreme fright the government is in. Italy too has witnessed a mass outbreak in Turin. Most important, however, is the mutiny in the German navy. One can imagine the enormous difficulties of a revolution in a country like Germany, especially under present conditions. It cannot be doubted that the mutiny in the German navy is indicative of the great crisis – the maturing of the world revolution. While our chauvinists, who are advocating the defeat of Germany, demand a revolt of the German workers immediately, we Russian revolutionary internationalists know from the experience of 1905-17 that a more impressive sign of the growth of revolution than a mutiny among the troops cannot be imagined.

Just think what our position is now in the eyes of the German revolutionaries. They can say to us: We have only Liebknecht who openly called for a revolution. His voice has been stifled in a convict prison. We have not a single newspaper which openly explains the necessity for a revolution; we have not got freedom of assembly. We have not a single Soviet of Workers' or Soldiers' Deputies. Our voice barely reaches the real, broad masses. Yet we made an attempt at revolt, although our chance was only one in a hundred. But you Russian revolutionary internationalists have behind you a half-year of freedom of agitation; you have a score of newspapers; you have a number of Soviets of Workers' and Soldiers' Deputies; you have gained the upper hand in the Soviets of both capitals; you have on your side the entire Baltic Fleet and all the Russian troops in Finland. And still you do not respond to our call for revolt, you do not overthrow your imperialist, Kerensky, although the chances are a hundred to one that your revolt will be successful.

Yes, we shall be real traitors to the International if, at such a moment and under such favorable conditions, we respond to such a call of the German revolutionaries with... mere resolutions:

Add to this, as we all perfectly well know, that the plotting and conspiracy of the international imperialists against the Russian revolution are rapidly growing. International imperialism is coming more and more to the idea of stifling the revolution at all costs, stifling it both by military measures and by a peace made at the expense of Russia. It is this that is making the crisis in the world socialist revolution so acute, and that is rendering our procrastination in the matter of revolt particularly dangerous – I would almost say criminal.

Take, further, the internal situation of Russia. The petty-bourgeois conciliationist parties, which expressed the naive confidence of the masses in Kerensky and in the imperialists in general, are absolutely bankrupt, their collapse is complete. The vote cast against coalition by the Soviet *curia* at the Democratic Conference; the vote cast against coalition by a *majority* of the local Soviets of Peasants' Deputies (in spite of their Central Soviet, where Avksentyev and other friends of Kerensky's are installed); the elections in Moscow, where the working-class population has the closest ties with the peasantry, and where-over 49 per cent voted for the Bolsheviks (and among the soldiers fourteen thousand out of seventeen thousand) – does this not signify that the confidence of the masses in Kerensky and in those who are compromising with Kerensky and his friends has totally collapsed? Can one imagine any way in which the masses could say more clearly to the Bolsheviks than they did by this vote: "Lead us, we shall follow you"?

Are we, who have won the majority of the people over to our side, and who have gained the Soviets of both capitals, to wait? What for? For Kerensky and his Kornilovist generals to surrender Petrograd to the Germans, and thus enter directly or indirectly, overtly or covertly, into a conspiracy with both Buchanan and Wilhelm for the purpose of completely stifling the Russian revolution?

By the Moscow vote and by the elections to the Soviets, the people have expressed their confidence in us, but that is not all. There are signs of growing apathy and indifference. That is easily understood. It implies not the ebb of the revolution, as the Cadets and their henchmen vociferate, but the ebb of confidence in resolutions and elections. In a revolution, the masses demand of the leading parties action, not words; they demand victories in the struggle, not talk. The moment is approaching when the people may conceive the opinion that the Bolsheviks are no better than the others, since they were unable to act when confidence was placed in them....

The peasant insurrection is spreading over the whole country. It is perfectly clear that the Cadets and their satellites are minimizing it in every way and are representing it to be nothing but "pogroms" and "anarchy." That lie is refuted by the fact that in the centers of revolt the land is beginning to be handed over to the peasants. "Pogroms" and "anarchy" have never led to such splendid political results! The tremendous strength of the peasant revolt is shown by the fact that the compromisers and the Socialist-Revolutionaries of the

Dyelo Naroda, and *even* Breshko-Breshkovskaya, have begun to talk of giving the land to the peasants in order to stop the movement before it has engulfed them.

And are we to wait until the Cossack detachments of the Kornilovist Kerensky (who was recently exposed as a Kornilovist by the Socialist-Revolutionaries themselves) succeed in suppressing this peasant uprising *piecemeal?*

Apparently, many leaders of our Party have failed to note the specific meaning of the slogan which we all adopted and which we have repeated endlessly. The slogan is "All power to the Soviets." There were periods, there were moments during the half-year of the revolution, when this slogan did not imply insurrection. Perhaps those periods and those moments blinded some of our comrades and led them to forget that now, at least since the middle of September, this slogan for us too has become *equivalent to a call for insurrection.*

There can be no shadow of doubt on this point. *Dyelo Naroda* recently explained this "in a popular way," when it said, "Kerensky will never submit!" What a question!

The slogan "All power to the Soviets" is a call for revolt. And the blame will be wholly and entirely ours, if we, who for months have been calling upon the masses to revolt and repudiate compromise, fail to lead those masses to revolt on the eve of the collapse of the revolution, after the masses have expressed their confidence in us.

The Cadets and compromisers are trying to scare us by citing the example of July 16-18 (3-5), by pointing to the intensified agitation of the Black Hundreds, and so forth. But if any mistake was made on July 16-18, it was that we did not seize power. I think that then there was no mistake, for at that time we were not yet in a majority. But now it would be a fatal mistake, worse than a mistake. The spread of Black Hundred agitation is easily understood; it is an aggravation of extremes in an atmosphere of a developing proletarian and peasant revolution. But to use this as an argument *against* revolt is ridiculous, for the impotence of the Black Hundred hirelings of the capitalists, *the impotence of the Black Hundreds in a fight,* does not even require proof. In a fight, Kornilov and Kerensky can rely only upon the support of the "Savage Division" and the Cossacks. And now demoralization has set in even among the Cossacks; besides, the peasants are threatening them with civil war within their Cossack territories.

I am writing these lines on Sunday, October 21 (8). You will read them not earlier than October 23 (10). I have heard from a comrade who passed through here that people traveling on the Warsaw railroad say, "Kerensky is leading the Cossacks on Petrograd!" This is quite probable, and it will be entirely our fault if we do not verify it most carefully and do not make a study of the strength and distribution of *the Kornilovist troops of the second draft.*

Kerensky has again brought Kornilovist troops into the vicinity of Petrograd in order to prevent the power of government from passing into the hands of the Soviets, in order to prevent such a government from proposing an immediate peace, in order to prevent all the land from being immediately handed over to the peasantry and in order to surrender Petrograd to the Germans, while he himself escapes to Moscow! That is the slogan of the insurrection which we must circulate as widely as possible and which will meet with a tremendous response.

We must not wait for the All-Russian Congress of Soviets, which the Central Executive Committee may delay even until November. We must not procrastinate and permit Kerensky to bring up more Kornilovist troops. Finland, the fleet and Reval are represented at the Congress of Soviets. These together can start an immediate movement on Petrograd against the Kornilovist regiments, a movement of the fleet, artillery, machine-guns and two or three army corps, such as have shown, for instance in Vyborg, the intensity of their hatred for the Kornilovist generals, with whom Kerensky is again in collusion.

It would be a great mistake were we to fail to seize the opportunity of immediately smashing the Kornilovist regiments of the second draft for fear that, by moving into Petrograd, the Baltic Fleet would allegedly expose the front to the Germans. The Kornilovist slanderers will say this, for they will tell any lie, but it is not worthy of revolutionaries to allow themselves to be frightened by lies and slander. Kerensky will deliver Petrograd to the Germans, that is now as clear as daylight. No assertion to the contrary can shake our utter conviction that that is so, for it follows from the entire course of events and from Kerensky's entire policy.

Kerensky and the Kornilovists will surrender Petrograd to the Germans. And in order to save Petrograd, Kerensky must be overthrown and the power seized by the *Soviets of both capitals.* These Soviets will immediately propose a peace to all the nations and will thereby fulfil their duty to the German revolutionaries. They will thereby also be taking a decisive step towards frustrating the criminal conspiracies against the Russian revolution, the conspiracies of international imperialism.

Only the immediate movement of the Baltic Fleet, the Finnish troops, and Reval and Kronstadt against the Kornilovist troops quartered near Petrograd can save the Russian and the world revolutions. Such a movement has ninety-nine chances out of a hundred of leading within a few days to the surrender of a part of the Cossack troops, to the complete defeat of the other part, and to the overthrow of Kerensky, for the workers and the soldiers of both capitals will support such a movement.

Verily, procrastination is like unto death.

The slogan "All power to the Soviets" is a slogan of insurrection. Whoever uses this slogan without having grasped and pondered on this will have only himself to blame. And insurrection must be treated as an art. I insisted on this during the Democratic Conference and I insist on it now; because *that* is what Marxism teaches us, and it is what is being taught us by the present situation in Russia and in the world generally.

It is not a question of voting, of attracting the "Left Socialist-Revolutionaries," of additional provincial Soviets, or of a congress of these Soviets. It is a question of insurrection, which can and must be decided by Petrograd, Moscow, Helsingfors, Kronstadt, Vyborg and Reval. *In the vicinity of Petrograd* and in Petrograd itself – that is where the insurrection can, and must, be decided on and effected. It must be effected as earnestly as possible, with as much preparation as possible, as quickly as possible and as energetically as possible.

The fleet, Kronstadt, Vyborg, Reval, can and must advance on Petrograd; they must smash the Kornilov regiments, rouse both the capitals, start a mass agitation for a government which will immediately give the land to the peasants and immediately make proposals for peace, and must overthrow Kerensky's government and establish such a government.

Verily, procrastination is like unto death.

V. I. Lenin, "A Letter to the Bolshevik Comrades Attending the Regional Congress of the Soviets of the Northern Region," *Selected Works*, Vol. VI.'

How, then, could such a miracle happen as the victory of the Bolsheviks, who received one-fourth of the votes, as against the petty-bourgeois democrats who had formed a coalition with the bourgeoisie and who together with it secured three-fourths of the votes?

For to deny the fact of victory now, after two years' assistance by the Entente – the universally powerful Entente – to all adversaries of the Bolsheviks, is simply laughable.

This precisely is the point, that the furious political hatred of those who have suffered defeat, including all the adherents of the Second International, does not permit them even seriously to pose the most interesting historical and political question of the causes of the victory of the Bolsheviks. This precisely is the point: that here there has been a miracle only from the point of view of vulgar petty-bourgeois democracy, the whole depth of the ignorance and prejudices of which democracy is being brought to light by this question and the answer to it.

From the point of view of the class struggle and of socialism, which has been abandoned by the Second International, the question is decided without dispute. The Bolsheviks were victorious in the first place because they had behind them the vast majority of the proletariat, and within it the most class-conscious, energetic, revolutionary section, the real vanguard of this foremost class.

Let us take both capitals, Petrograd and Moscow. The aggregate number of votes cast there for the Constituent Assembly was 1,765,100. Of these the

S.R.'s received	218,000 votes
Bolsheviks received	837,000 votes
Cadets received	515,400 votes

No matter how much the petty-bourgeois democrats, who call themselves socialists and social-democrats (the Chernovs, Kautskys, Longuets, MacDonalds & Co.) would break their foreheads prostrating themselves before such deities as "equality," "universal suffrage," "democracy," "pure democracy," or "consistent democracy," this will not cause the economic and political fact of the *inequality* of town and country to disappear.

This is an unavoidable fact under capitalism in general, and during the transition from capitalism to communism in particular.

The town cannot be on a par with the countryside. The countryside cannot be on a par with the town in the historical conditions of this epoch. The town inevitably *leads* the countryside. The countryside inevitably *follows the town.* The question is only *what class* of the "urban" classes will be able to lead the countryside, will be able to cope with this task, and what forms this *leadership of the town* will take.

In November, 1917, the Bolsheviks had the overwhelming majority of the proletariat behind them. The party that was competing with them among the proletariat, the Mensheviks, was badly beaten at that time (9 million votes against 1.4 million, if we are to add to the 668,000 the 700,000-800,000 from the Trans-Caucasus). And this party was beaten in the fifteen years of struggle (1903-1917) which had *hardened,* enlightened, organized the vanguard of the proletariat by *hammering* out of it a really revolutionary vanguard. And the first revolution, 1905, prepared the further development, determined *in practice* the mutual relations between the two parties, played the role of a general rehearsal of the great events of 1917-1919.

The petty-bourgeois democrats, who call themselves "socialists" of the Second International, like to divorce themselves from a very serious historical question by sugary phrases about the usefulness of the "unity" of the proletariat. Behind this sugary phrasemongering they forget the historical fact of the *accumulation of opportunism* in the labor movement from 1871 to 1914; they forget (or do not want) to *think* about the reasons for the crash of opportunism in August, 1914, about the reasons for the split in international socialism in 1914-1917.

Without *most* seriously preparing, from every angle, the *revolutionary* section of the proletariat to drive out and suppress opportunism, it would be foolish even to think of a dictatorship of the proletariat. This lesson of the Russian Revolution ought to be held up to the noses of the leaders of the "Independent" German Social Democrats, of French socialism and the like who to-day want to wriggle out of it by a verbal recognition of the dictatorship of the proletariat.

Furthermore. The Bolsheviks had behind them not only the majority of the proletariat, not only the *revolutionary* vanguard of the proletariat, hardened in the long and stubborn fight against opportunism. They had, if one may be permitted to use a military term, powerful "crack troops" in the capitals.

To have an overwhelming preponderance of forces at the decisive moment at the decisive point – this "law" of military success is also a law of political success, especially in the cruel, seething war of classes which is called revolution.

The capitals or in general the biggest trading and industrial centers (here in Russia these terms coincided, but they do not always coincide) to a considerable degree decide the political fate of the people, of course only if the centers are supported by sufficient local, rural forces, though this be not immediate support.

In both capitals, in both the trading and industrial centers, most important for Russia, the Bolsheviks had an overwhelming, decisive preponderance of forces. We had here *almost four times* as many votes as the S.R.'s. We had here *more than the S.R.'s and the Cadets taken together*. Besides, our opponents were split up, since the "coalition" between the Cadets and the S.R.'s and Mensheviks (both in Petrograd and Moscow the Mensheviks had altogether 3 per cent of the votes) had been utterly compromised among the toiling masses. At that time there could be no talk of any *real* unity between S.R.'s and Mensheviks and the Cadets against us.[*] As is well known, even the leaders of the S.R.'s and Mensheviks, who are a hundred times nearer to the idea of a *bloc* with the Cadets than the S.R. and Menshevik workers and peasants – even these leaders thought (and dickered with us) about a coalition with the Bolsheviks *without* Cadets!

The capitals we conquered in October-November, 1917, *for certain,* having an overwhelming preponderance of forces and the most substantial political preparation, both in the sense of collecting, concentrating, training, testing, hardening the Bolshevik "armies" as well as in the sense of disintegrating, rendering impotent, disuniting, demoralizing the "armies" of the "enemy."

And having the opportunity of winning, as a certainty, by a quick, decisive blow, both capitals, both centers of the entire capitalist machine of the state (both with respect to economics and politics) we, despite the frantic resistance of the bureaucracy and "intelligentsia," sabotage, etc., were able, with the aid of the central apparatus of the state power, to *prove* to the toiling and non-proletarian masses *by deeds* that the proletariat is their only reliable ally, friend and leader.

---

[*] It is of interest to note the unity and coherence of the Party of the proletariat disclosed by the data quoted above at a time when the parties of the petty bourgeoisie and the party of the bourgeoisie were highly scattered.

But before passing on to this, the most important, question, the question of the relationship between the proletariat and the non-proletarian toiling masses, one ought likewise to dwell upon the *army*.

At the time of the imperialist war, the army absorbed in its entirety the flower of the popular forces; and if the opportunist scoundrels of the Second International (not only the social chauvinists, *i.e.*, those who went over directly to the side of the "defense of the fatherland" – the Scheidemanns and the Renaudels – but also the "centrists") by their words and their deeds strengthened the subordination of the army to the leadership of the imperialist robbers of the German as well as the Anglo-French group, the real proletarian revolutionaries never forgot the words of Marx which were uttered in 1870: "The bourgeoisie will teach the proletariat how to handle arms!" Only the Austro-German and Anglo-Franco-Russian betrayers of socialism could speak of the "defense of the fatherland" in the imperialist (*i.e.*, predatory on both sides) war; but the proletarian revolutionaries turned their whole attention (beginning with August, 1914) to the revolutionization of the army, to using it *against* the imperialist pirates of the bourgeoisie, to converting the unjust and predatory war between two groups of imperialist robbers into the just and lawful war of the proletarians and the oppressed toiling masses of each country against "its own" "national" bourgeoisie.

The traitors to socialism *did not prepare* for 1914-17 the use of the army *against* the imperialist governments of *each* nation.

The Bolsheviks did make such preparation by the whole of their propaganda, agitation, their illegally organized work since August, 1914. Of course the traitors to socialism, the Scheidemanns and Kautskys of all nations, would have none of this, ranting about the *disintegration* of the army by Bolshevik agitation, while we are *proud* of the fact that we did our duty by disintegrating the forces of our class enemy, by winning away *from him* the armed masses of the workers and peasants *for the struggle* against the exploiters.

The results of our work expressed themselves also in the vote at the elections for the Constituent Assembly in November, 1917, in which (the voting) the army in Russia also took part.

Here are the main results of this vote, as given by N. V. Svyatitsky:

Number of Votes (in thousands) Cast in November, 1917, at the Elections to the Constituent Assembly

Army and Navy units	For the S.R.'s	For the Bolsheviks	For the Cadets	For the national and other groups	Total
Northern Front	240.0	480.0	?	60.0[*]	780.0
Western Front	180.6	653.4	16.7	125.2	976.0
South-Western Front	402.9	300.1	13.7	290.6	1007.4
Rumanian Front	679.4	167.0	21.4	260.7	1128.6
Caucasian Front	360.0	60.0	?	....	420.0
Baltic Fleet	....	(120.0)[*]	...	....	(120.0)[*]
Black Sea Fleet	22.2	10.8	...	19.5[†]	(52.5)
Total	1885.1	1671.3 + (120.0)[*] 1791.3	51.8 +?	756.0	4364.5 +(120.0)[*] +?

The totals show: For the S.R.'s – 1,885,100 votes; for the Bolsheviks – 1,671,300. And if we add to the latter the (approximately) 120,000 cast by the Baltic Fleet, we get 1,791,300 votes for the Bolsheviks.

Consequently, the Bolsheviks received *a few less* than the S.R.'s.

The army was consequently already in October-November, 1917, *half Bolshevik.*

Without this we would not have been victorious.

But while getting almost half the votes in the army in general, we had the overwhelming majority at the fronts *nearest to the captals* and in general stationed at not too great a distance. If we deduct the Caucasian front, the Bolsheviks have in general a lead over the S.R.'s. And if we take the Northern and Western fronts, the Bolsheviks get *over one million votes* as against 420,000 for the S.R.'s.

Consequently, in the army the Bolsheviks as early as Novem-

---

[*] Approximate figure: 2 Bolsheviks were elected. N. V. Svyatitsky counts 60,000 votes on the average for every person elected. For this reason I set down 120,000.

[†] No information is given on what party received 19,500 votes from the Black Sea Fleet. The remaining figures of this column evidently represent almost exclusively Ukrainian Socialists, since 10 Ukrainian Socialists and 1 Social-Democrat (*i.e.,* a Menshevik) were elected.

ber, 1917, likewise had *political "shock troops"* which assured them of an overwhelming preponderance of forces at the decisive point at the decisive moment. There can be no talk of any resistance on the part of the army to the October Revolution of the proletariat, to the conquest of political power by the proletariat, when the Bolsheviks had a towering majority at the Northern and Western fronts, and at the other fronts remote from the center had the time and the opportunity *to win the peasants away from the party of the S.R.'s,* of which we will speak later.

On the basis of the Constituent Assembly election data we have learned three conditions for the victory of Bolshevism: (1) the overwhelming majority of the proletariat; (2) almost half of the army; (3) the overwhelming preponderance of forces at the decisive moment at the decisive points, *viz.,* in the capitals and at the army fronts near the center.

But these conditions could have produced only the most short-lived and unstable victory if the Bolsheviks had been unable to attract to their side the majority of the non-proletarian toiling masses, winning them away for themselves from the S.R.'s and the other petty-bourgeois parties.

Herein lies the gist of the matter.

And the main cause of the failure of the "Socialists" (read "petty-bourgeois democrats") of the Second International to understand the dictatorship of the proletariat consists in their failure to understand that

the state power in the hands of one class, the proletariat, can and must become an instrument for attracting the non-proletarian toiling masses to the side of the proletariat, an instrument for winning these masses away from the bourgeoisie and the petty-bourgeois parties.

V. I. Lenin, "The Elections to the Constituent Assembly and the Dictatorship of the Proletariat," 1919, *Collected Works,* Vol. XXIV, Russian edition.

www.ingramcontent.com/pod-product-compliance
Lightning Source LLC
Chambersburg PA
CBHW070150290526
45789CB00002B/701